D1394703

The SETTLEMENT OF AUSTRALIA
FROM COLONY TO NATION

CHRISTINE HATT

Evans

EVANS BROTHERS LIMITED

Published by Evans Brothers Limited
2A Portman Mansions
Chiltern Street
London
W1M ILE

First published in 1999
Printed in Spain by Grafo S.A. - Bilbao.

British Library Cataloguing in Publication Data

Hatt, Christine
  The settlement of Australia. - (History in writing)
  1.Australia - History - 1788-1901 - Juvenile literature
  I.Title
  994'.02

  ISBN 023751883X

Design – Neil Sayer
Editorial – Nicola Barber
Maps – Nick Hawken
Consultant – Professor Carl Bridge, Sir Robert Menzies Centre
for Australian Studies, University of London
Production – Jenny Mulvanny

Title page picture: Raising the Union Jack flag in Sydney
on 26 January 1788

Border: Fish pattern based on an Aboriginal design

ACKNOWLEDGEMENTS

For permission to reproduce copyright pictorial material, the author and publishers gratefully acknowledge the following:
Cover (left) Dixson Galleries, State Library of New South Wales/Bridgeman Art Library (centre) Mary Evans Picture Library (right) Mary Evans Picture Library (bottom right) National Library of Australia, Canberra, Australia/Bridgeman Art Library **Title page** Commonwealth Club, London/Bridgeman Art Library **page 6** Mitchell Library, State Library of New South Wales/ Bridgeman Art Library **page 8** National Library of Australia, Canberra/Bridgeman Art Library **page 9** (top) Fritz Prenzel/Bruce Coleman Collection (bottom) B Norman/Ancient Art and Architecture **page 10** Mary Evans Picture Library **page 11** (top right) Mary Evans Picture Library (bottom) Mary Evans Picture Library **page 12** Private Collection/Bridgeman Art Library **page 13** (top left) British Library, London/Bridgeman Art Library (middle right) Victoria Art Gallery, Bath and North East Somerset Council/Bridgeman Art Library (bottom) Mary Evans Picture Library **page 14** (top right) Mary Evans Picture Library (bottom) Mary Evans/Bruce Castle Museum Collection **page 15** Mary Evans Picture Library **page 16** (top) Agnew & Sons, London/Bridgeman Art Library (bottom) Mary Evans Picture Library **page 17** Mitchell Library, State Library of New South Wales/ Bridgeman Art Library **page 19** Mitchell Library, State Library of New South Wales/Bridgeman Art Library **page 20** (top) Mary Evans Picture Library (bottom) Mary Evans Picture Library **page 21** Mary Evans Picture Library **page 22** Commonwealth Club, London/Bridgeman Art Library **page 24** Mary Evans Picture Library **page 25** National Library of Australia, Canberra/ Bridgeman Art Library **page 26** Mary Evans Picture Library **page 27** Mitchell Library, State Library of New South Wales/Bridgeman Art Library **page 28** (top) Dixson Galleries, State Library of New South Wales/Bridgeman Art Library (bottom) Mitchell Library, State Library of New South Wales **page 29** (top) Royal Geographical Society, London/Bridgeman Art Library (bottom) National Library of Australia, Canberra/Bridgeman Art Library **page 30** Dixson Galleries, State Library of New South Wales/Bridgeman Art Library **page 31** Mitchell Library, State Library of New South Wales/Bridgeman Art Library **page 32** (top) Mitchell Library, State Library of New South Wales/Bridgeman Art Library (bottom) Mitchell Library, State Library of New South Wales/Bridgeman Art Library **page 33** National Library of Australia, Canberra, Australia/Bridgeman Art Library **page 34** (top) Mary Evans Picture Library (bottom) National Library of Australia, Canberra, Australia/Bridgeman Art Library **page 35** Mary Evans Picture Library **page 36** (top) Mary Evans Picture Library (bottom) Mary Evans Picture Library **page 37** Mary Evans Picture Library **page 38** (top and bottom) Dixson Galleries, State Library of New South Wales/Bridgeman Art Library (top) **page 39** Mary Evans Picture Library **page 41** Mitchell Library, State Library of New South Wales/Bridgeman Art Library **page 43** National Library of Australia, Canberra, Australia/Bridgeman Art Library **page 44** (top and bottom) Mary Evans Picture Library **page 45** Mary Evans Picture Library **page 46** Mary Evans Picture Library **page 48** (top

right) Birmingham Museums and Art Gallery/Bridgeman Art Library (bottom left) Dixson Galleries, State Library of New South Wales/Bridgeman Art Library **page 49** Mitchell Library, State Library of New South Wales/Bridgeman Art Library **page 50** Mary Evans Picture Library **page 51** (top) Robert Francis/Robert Harding Picture Library (middle) Mitchell Library, State Library of New South Wales/Bridgeman Art Library **page 52** National Library of Australia, Canberra, Australia/Bridgeman Art Library **page 53** Mary Evans Picture Library **page 54** Mary Evans Picture Library **page 55** (left) Mary Evans Picture Library (right) Mary Evans Picture Library **page 56** National Library of Australia, Canberra, Australia/Bridgeman Art Library **page 57** (left) Mary Evans Picture Library (right) Bruce Willis/Hutchison Library **page 58** (left) Christine Osborne Pictures **page 59** Penny Tweedie/Panos Pictures

For permission to reproduce copyright material for the documents, the author and publisher gratefully acknowledge the following:

page 9 From Australian Legendary Tales, collected by K Langloh Parker, first published in 1953 by Angus and Robertson Publishers. Reprinted by permission of Harper Collins Publishers **page 11** From The Voyages of Captain James Cook Round the World, Selected from his Journals and Edited by Christopher Lloyd, first published in 1949 by The Cresset Press **page 17** (bottom) From The Penguin Book of Australian Ballads, Ed. By Rusel Ward (Penguin Book, Ringwood, Vic., 1965), 24-6 **page 21** From The Crimes of the First Fleet Convicts, first published in 1953 by Angus and Robertson Publishers. Reprinted by permission of Harper Collins Publishers. **page 27** (top) From Australian Colonists by Ken Inglis, published in 1993 by Melbourne University Press (bottom) From The Fatal Shore by Robert Hughes, published by The Harvill Press **page 45** (top) From Australian Colonists by Ken Inglis, published in 1993 by Melbourne University Press (bottom) From Annabella Boswell's Journal, first published in 1965 by Angus and Robertson Publishers. Reprinted by permission of Harper Collins Publishers **page 49** (top) From The Eureka Stockade by Raffaello Carboni, published in 1963 by Melbourne University Press (bottom) From A Lady's Visit to the Gold Diggings of Australia in 1852-1853, published in 1963 by Angus and Robertson Publishers. Reprinted by permission of Harper Collins Publishers. **page 59** (top) From Annabella Boswell's Journal, first published in 1965 by Angus and Robertson Publishers. Reprinted by permission of Harper Collins Publishers (middle) From The Fatal Shore by Robert Hughes, published by The Harvill Press

Every effort has been made to trace copyright holders but in some cases this has not proved possible. The publisher will be happy to rectify any such errors or omissions in future reprints and/or new editions.

CONTENTS

LOOKING AT DOCUMENTS

The theme of this book is the peopling of the Australian continent by foreign settlers from 1788 until the Commonwealth of Australia was established in 1901. It examines the conditions in Great Britain, Ireland and elsewhere that forced or persuaded people to begin new lives on the other side of the world. It looks at the many hardships that the immigrants endured and the ways of life they developed. It considers the catastrophic effect of their arrival on Australia's original settlers, the Aborigines. Finally, it charts the birth of a distinctive new nation.

The first European settlers in Australia were convicts who had been transported (deported) from Britain. With them were the naval officers and marines who set up and ran the penal colony. But the population soon grew and changed. Convicts who had finished their sentences usually stayed in the colony and became semi-respectable Emancipists (see pages 26-7). In the 19th century, many free settlers arrived, attracted by land, gold or adventure. By the time transportation ended in 1868, a settlement intended only for criminals had developed a life of its own.

To bring this story to life, *The Settlement of Australia* uses a wide range of documents. These include court reports, journals of naval officers and explorers, letters of early settlers and extracts from novels. To make the documents easier to read, we have printed them in modern type. However, you will find photographs of original documents alongside several of the extracts. Difficult or old-fashioned words or phrases are explained in the labels around the documents.

As you are looking at the documents, it is important to think about their origins. When were they written – at a time when most people thought transportation was acceptable, or when they were starting to ask whether it was either effective or humane? Where were they written – in Australia, so likely to contain realistic descriptions, or abroad, so often full of mistaken ideas? Finally, who wrote them – people expressing an honest opinion or people with selfish motives? Such questions will help you to work out how reliable a document is likely to be. But remember that no single document can provide a complete picture of any situation, whether past or present.

On these pages are a few extracts from the documents used in this book. They have been selected to give you an idea of the variety of documents included, and to explain how and why some were written.

The British government and monarchy issued many official documents relating to their Australian colony. The first Governor of New South Wales, Captain Arthur Phillip, was given instructions in this commission from King George III (see page 17).

You are to endeavour by every possible means to open an intercourse with the natives... enjoining all our subjects to live in amity and kindness with them.

Captain Arthur Phillip

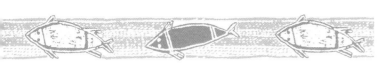

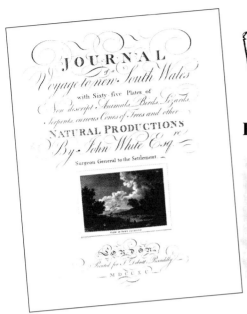

Many surviving diaries and journals contain vivid eye-witness reports of Australia's early years. This extract is from the journal of the surgeon on the First Fleet, John White (see page 19).

My first care was to keep the men... out of the rain; and I never suffered the convicts to come upon deck when it rained, as they had neither linen nor clothing sufficient to make themselves dry and comfortable after getting wet...

The British courts kept detailed reports of convict trials. This is one of three in the book that feature criminals who sailed on the First Fleet to Australia in 1788 (see page 21).

You can find out what **Peruke** means on page 21.

Name: Henry Abrams
Age: 26
Place of Trial: Chelmsford, Essex
The court report charged Abrams with three offences of highway robbery. During the first he was said to have stolen the following:
'one linen Ruffled Shirt of the value of five shillings one Muslin Neckcloth of the value of 12d. one pair of Men's Leather Breeches of the value of 10 shillings one Man's **Peruke** of the value of 2 shillings one stuff Bag of the value of 2 shillings and one pair of Leather Boot Garters of the value of 12d. one Piece of Gold Coin...called a half Guinea...and fifteen shillings in monies numbered.'
Sentence: 7 years' transportation.

Newspapers can often provide important information about historical events. This letter, which describes how Europeans treated Aborigines, appeared in an 1880 edition of *The Queenslander* (see page 43).

This, in plain language, is how we deal with the aborigines: On occupying new territory the aboriginal inhabitants are treated exactly in the same way as the wild beasts or birds the settlers may find there. Their lives and their property, the nets, canoes, and weapons which represent as much labor to them as the stock and buildings of the white settler, are held by the Europeans as being at their absolute disposal.

ORIGINS
AUSTRALIAN ABORIGINES

People first arrived in Australia about 50,000 years ago, during the last Ice Age. At that time, the freezing temperatures had turned vast volumes of sea water into ice, lowering sea levels and exposing large areas of the sea bed. These exposed areas of land often formed bridges between islands and continents. For example, it became possible to reach areas far to the south of China on foot, then make a sea crossing of only 60 km to north Australia (see map), and this is what many groups of people did.

A painting by a European artist of an Aboriginal ceremony known as a *corroboree*. The Aborigines have held these sacred ceremonies for thousands of years.

Australia's first inhabitants gradually spread out, reaching the far south by about 25,000 years ago. Most made their homes near lakes, rivers and seashores, where there was plenty of fish and shellfish to eat.

But as the Ice Age began to end, about 10,000 years ago, the rising ocean swallowed up much of the coast and more groups moved inland. At the same time the land bridges disappeared.

The Aborigines developed their own unique ways of life. They survived by gathering plants, fishing and hunting. They also learned how to use fire for hunting and to control plant growth. Few groups stayed in one place all year round. Most were semi-nomadic, moving around within a fixed territory to find food.

Aborigines developed a wide range of tools and weapons, such as adzes, spears and boomerangs. By about 3000

Map labels:

CHINA

PHILIPPINES

Pacific Ocean

BORNEO

SUMATRA

N

JAVA   INDONESIA

NEW GUINEA

Probable migration routes

Ice Age coastline

Modern-day coastline

Land bridges

AUSTRALIA

ANCIENT MIGRATION ROUTES

TASMANIA

One land bridge joined Borneo and other Southeast Asian islands to China. Another linked Australia to New Guinea.

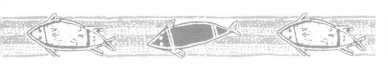

years ago, they had established a network of trade routes across Australia. People from many tribes met on its paths to exchange goods such as red ochre (a type of mineral used to make paint) and shells. Religious beliefs were also passed from tribe to tribe in this way.

By the time Captain Cook reached Australia in 1770 (see pages 10-11), at least 750,000 Aborigines lived there. They were divided into about 600 tribal groups and spoke hundreds of languages. The great majority had never met anyone from outside their own continent.

This Aboriginal rock painting of a kangaroo is from the Northern Territory in Australia.

THE DREAMTIME

The Aborigines lived in many different environments, from the humid rainforests of the north to the arid central deserts. But all believed that the world was formed during a sacred era in the distant past known as the 'Dreamtime', or 'Dreaming'. In the Dreamtime, the Aborigines' spirit ancestors walked on Earth, creating its natural features, plants, animals and people. When their work was over, the spirits disappeared from view. However, according to Aboriginal beliefs, they are invisibly present in land, trees, water and sky, and their great power can still be felt.

Rock engraving is the oldest form of Aboriginal art, dating back 30,000 years or more. This example is from Ewaninga, near Alice Springs.

Aborigines celebrate and relive the Dreamtime in ceremonies, songs and stories. This Dreamtime tale explains how the sun was made.

Modern experts confirm that giant kangaroos, wombats and other marsupials roamed Australia until about 15,000 years ago.

Native companion is used here to mean 'crane' (a type of bird).

The **Murrumbidgee** is a river in southeast Australia.

For a long time there was no sun, only a moon and stars. That was before there were men on the earth, only birds and beasts, all of which were many sizes larger than they are now. One day Dinewan the emu and Brolga the native companion were on a large plain near the Murrumbidgee. There they were, quarrelling and fighting. Brolga, in her rage, rushed to the nest of Dinewan and seized from it one of the huge eggs, which she threw with all her force up to the sky. There it broke on a heap of firewood, which burst into a flame as the yellow yolk spilt all over it, which flame lit up the world below... A good spirit who lived in the sky saw how bright and beautiful the earth looked when lit up by this blaze. He thought it would be a good thing to make a fire every day; which from that time he has done...

EUROPEAN EXPLORATION

In about AD150, the Greek-born scholar Ptolemy wrote a book called *Geography*. In it, he stated that there was a huge, undiscovered land south of Europe and Asia that balanced these northern continents. The idea of the 'South Land' (*Terra Australis* in Latin) was born.

From the 15th century onwards, many explorers set out in search of land and riches. They knew about Terra Australis, but neither the Portuguese nor the Spanish could find this fabled region. However, Dutch sailors working in the area for the Dutch East India Company, a trading organisation, did discover a new land. In 1606, Willem Jansz's ship, the *Duyfken*, arrived on Australia's north coast. In 1616, Dirck Hartog's *Eendracht* reached the west.

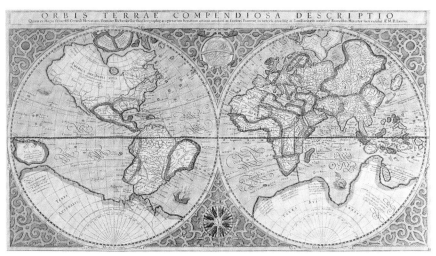

This map, by the famous cartographer Gerardus Mercator, dates from 1587. It shows the vast 'South Land' (Terra Australis) that people then believed lay in the southern half of the world.

The Dutch did not call their discovery 'Australia' but 'New Holland'. In 1642, Anthony van Diemen, head of the Dutch East India Company in Batavia (now Jakarta), launched an expedition to explore New Holland more fully. But the voyage's leader, Abel Tasman, steered too far south and the expedition landed on a different shore. Tasman named this island Van Diemen's Land (now Tasmania). In 1644, Tasman led another expedition, along Australia's north coast. However, he discovered no goods suitable for trading, so Dutch interest faded.

Terra Australis was believed to be a single vast landmass that covered the South Pole. By sailing south of New Holland, Tasman proved that this was not Terra Australis. Some people even began to doubt that such a place existed. In 1768, the British Admiralty sent Lieutenant (later Captain) James Cook to investigate. On his ship *Endeavour*, Cook searched the Pacific Ocean for the 'South Land' – without success – and mapped the coast of New Zealand. Then he decided to make his way home via New Holland.

THE EUROPEAN DISCOVERY OF AUSTRALIA

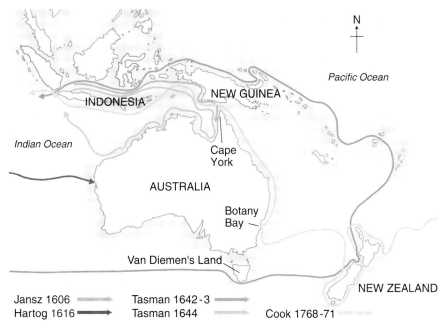

N

Pacific Ocean

INDONESIA

NEW GUINEA

Indian Ocean

Cape York

AUSTRALIA

Botany Bay

Van Diemen's Land

NEW ZEALAND

Jansz 1606
Hartog 1616
Tasman 1642-3
Tasman 1644
Cook 1768-71

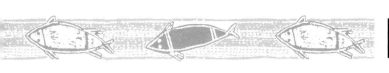
On 29 April 1770, Cook and his crew landed on the east coast of New Holland, at a place that became known as Botany Bay. In August they reached Cape York to the north. There they raised the Union Jack and claimed the east coast, which they called New South Wales, for Britain. At the time no one realised the significance of this event.

EARLY ARRIVALS

Some experts believe that outsiders reached Australia long before the Dutch arrived in 1606. There are unproven claims that the Chinese went there in the 15th century and the Portuguese in the 16th century. But all historians agree that men from the port of Makassar on the Indonesian island of Sulawesi regularly sailed to Australia's north coast as early as the 1500s. Their aim was to catch highly prized sea cucumbers.

William Dampier stands on the deck of his ship. Dampier was an English buccaneer who twice explored the west coast of New Holland, in 1688 and 1699. His book, *A New Voyage round the World* (1697), helped to stir up interest in the region.

Captain Cook (left) kept a journal of his 1768-71 voyage across the Pacific Ocean. This extract tells of the landing at Botany Bay.

Here, **natives** means 'Aborigines'.

Tupia was a Tahitian. Cook had mistakenly hoped that he might be able to interpret the language of the Aborigines.

A **musket** was a type of gun used from the 16th to the 18th centuries.

April 29 [1770] Saw, as we came in, on both points of the bay, several of the natives and a few huts... As we approached the shore they all made off, except two men, who seemed resolved to oppose our landing. As soon as I saw this, I ordered the boats to lay upon their oars, in order to speak to them; but this was to little purpose, for neither us nor Tupia could understand one word they said. We then threw some nails, beads etc., ashore, which they took up, and... I thought that they beckoned to us to come ashore; but... as soon as we put the boat in they again came to oppose us, upon which I fired a musket...

GEORGIAN BRITAIN

George I became king of Great Britain and Ireland in 1714. This marked the beginning of the Georgian era, which lasted until 1830. During that period, Cook sailed to Australia (see pages 10-11). But many other major changes also swept the kingdom and the wider world.

In 1714, most British people lived in the countryside. In many places, landowners continued the traditional practice of dividing their open fields into strips and renting them out to poor farmers. But new farming methods such as crop rotation were not effective on open ground, where plant diseases spread and animals strayed. So more landowners began to enclose their fields with hedges and fences. The results of this Agricultural Revolution were mixed. Crops thrived, but enclosure left many landless labourers with nowhere to farm or keep livestock.

The Industrial Revolution also began in the Georgian era. In the early 1700s, cloth and other goods were made in people's homes. From the 1760s, the invention of improved spinning and weaving machines made it possible to work more quickly. However, these new machines were too large to keep in houses and too heavy for people to operate. So factories were set up where new types of steam engine powered the looms. Steam also provided power for iron-making. Coal was needed to drive the engines, so coal-mining grew in importance too.

Changing conditions drove thousands of people into the towns. Many went to industrial centres, such as Manchester and Birmingham. Others made their way to London, where the population was already soaring. In 1700, the capital had about 500,000 inhabitants. By 1811, its population was over one million. Overcrowded, dirty slums quickly developed, where diseases such as typhus and cholera spread rapidly.

While many people faced extreme poverty, others grew richer. Professional people such as lawyers flourished.

Women and children at work in a textile mill in the 18th century. At this time, children were expected to work up to 16 hours a day.

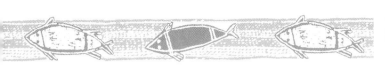

In the Georgian era, tea, sugar, spices and many other goods came to Britain by ship. In London, new docks were built to accommodate the increase in trade. The West India Docks (above) were completed in 1802.

Industrialists prospered as Britain's expanding empire provided raw materials as well as markets for finished goods. The rising middle classes wanted new homes where they could show off their wealth. Elegant town houses were built in cities such as Bath, as well as in London's West End.

The title page from an early 19th-century edition of Dickens's *Oliver Twist*

Impregnated with means 'filled with'.

Stock in trade means 'goods available for sale'.

UNREST IN IRELAND

The English first invaded Ireland in the 12th century and from that time the island was the site of many violent struggles. By the 18th century, the Protestant minority, who had been 'planted' on Irish territory by earlier monarchs, were in control – although still subject to the British parliament. The Roman Catholic majority was not represented in the Irish parliament and was kept in check by the harsh Penal Code. The bitter discontent felt at this state of affairs led to frequent unrest.

The Royal Crescent in Bath was designed by John Wood the Younger and completed in 1775. The elegant Crescent quickly became the city's most fashionable street.

English novelist Charles Dickens (1812-70) described London's slums in vivid detail. In this extract from *Oliver Twist*, Oliver enters the city's Saffron Hill area.

A dirtier or more wretched place he had never seen. The street was very narrow and muddy, and the air was impregnated with filthy odours. There were a good many small shops; but the only stock in trade appeared to be heaps of children, who, even at that time of night, were crawling in and out at the doors, or screaming from the inside. The sole places that seemed to prosper...were the public-houses ...Covered ways and yards, which here and there diverged from the main street, disclosed little knots of houses, where drunken men and women were positively wallowing in filth; and from several of the door-ways, great ill-looking fellows were cautiously emerging, bound, to all appearance, on no very well-disposed or harmless errands.

CRIME AND PUNISHMENT

Crime flourished in Georgian Britain. An 18th-century magistrate in the Tower Hamlets area of London estimated that about 115,000 inhabitants of the capital were engaged in illegal activities, from pickpocketing to murder. In the countryside, the poor poached and stole from the grand estates of the rich. Highwaymen such as Dick Turpin roamed the roads.

Crime prevention and detection were hampered by the lack of an official police force. Patrols by parish constables, nightwatchmen and beadles were largely ineffective. As the situation in London grew worse, one man took action. This was the novelist Henry Fielding, who was also a magistrate at the city's Bow Street court. In about 1750, he set up a group of thief-catchers, later known as the Bow Street Runners. But this small force could not tackle the city's crime wave alone.

The Georgian era was also a time of riots and other violent disturbances. From 1811 to about 1816, people known as Luddites broke into factories and smashed the new textile machines that they feared would put them out of work. The 'Swing riots' in 1830, named after the imaginary Captain Swing, were in part a protest against the Agricultural Revolution. Another cause of rebellion was dissatisfaction with Britain's political system. This feeling grew after the French Revolution, which began in 1789.

New Acts of Parliament were passed throughout the Georgian era in an attempt to control the rising tide of law-breaking. Crimes that would once have been

A member of a Bow Street Runner foot patrol. Other members of this early police force carried out their work on horseback.

punished by flogging or branding became hanging offences. Soon, over 150 crimes, including poaching, forgery and cutting down plants, led to the death sentence. Public executions, known as 'Hanging Matches', became common. At London's Tyburn gallows, thousands of people gathered to watch criminals die.

British justice was not without mercy. Many people who were condemned to death had their sentences changed. Instead of hanging they were imprisoned or transported – sent into exile overseas. But towards the end of the 18th century, the operation of the punishment system ran into trouble and changes had to be made (see pages 16-17).

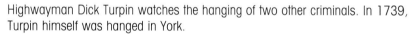
Highwayman Dick Turpin watches the hanging of two other criminals. In 1739, Turpin himself was hanged in York.

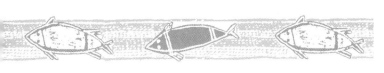
Jails in the 18th century were dirty, disease-ridden places. Jailers took no care of prisoners – their only duty was to keep them locked away. John Howard (1726-90) was so disgusted by prison conditions that he wrote a book to publicise them. In this extract from *The State of the Prisons in England and Wales* (1777), he describes London's notorious Newgate Jail.

This scene by William Hogarth shows a criminal (in the cart) on his way to the Tyburn gallows, while the crowd looks on in eager anticipation.

There are upon each of the three floors five cells: all vaulted, near nine feet high to the crown... In the upper part of each cell, is a window double grated... The doors are four inches thick. The strong stone wall is lined all round... with planks, studded with broad-headed nails. In each cell is a barrack-bedstead. I was told... that criminals who had affected an air of boldness during their trial, and appeared quite unconcerned at the pronouncing sentence upon them, were struck with horror, and shed tears when brought to these darksome solitary abodes.

London's law-breakers often specialised in particular offences. The following are just a few of the criminal categories listed in *London Labour and the London Poor* (1862) by Henry Mayhew.

... "Stook-buzzers," those who steal handkerchiefs.

... "Tail-Buzzers," those who dive into coat-pockets for sneezers (snuff-boxes,) skins and dummies (purses and pocket-books).

... "Star-glazers," or those who cut the panes out of shopwindows.

... "Sawney-Hunters," or those who go purloining bacon from cheese-mongers' shop-doors.

... "Noisy-Racket Men," or those who steal china and glass from outside of china shops...

... "Dead Lurkers," or those who steal coats and umbrellas from passages at dusk, or on Sunday afternoons.

... "Snow-Gatherers," or those who steal clean clothes off the hedges.

DESTINATION: BOTANY BAY

The transportation of criminals from Britain was rare until 1717, when it became government policy. Thousands of transportees were then shipped to British colonies in the Americas, where they worked on plantations. But after the American Revolution (1775-83), the newly independent USA refused to accept prisoners. Britain no longer had an outlet for its undesirables, and soon the jails were full.

The government's response was to pass the Hulks Act (1776). This made it legal to house convicts in hulks – old navy ships moored in rivers and off the coast. Convicts were expected to carry out heavy labour and their work gangs attracted hundreds of sightseers. But many politicians demanded that transportation begin again. The government agreed in principle and, in 1784, a new Transportation Act was passed. However, no one knew where the criminals should go.

In 1785, a committee headed by Lord Beauchamp was set up to investigate. West Africa was one potential site, but was rejected because of the risk of fatal diseases. Southwest Africa was another possibility, but also proved unsuitable. The committee then considered Botany Bay. Joseph Banks, who had been a botanist on Captain Cook's *Endeavour* expedition, had suggested the idea in 1779. After consulting him and James Matra,

A portrait of Joseph Banks, who recommended Botany Bay as a site for the new penal colony. James Cook originally called the area Sting Ray Bay, but renamed it because Banks found so many plants there.

another of Cook's fellow voyagers, the committee agreed. The government also approved because Britain's settlement of the region would help to keep out rival powers such as France.

The hulk *Defence* (left) and a convict hospital ship moored off Woolwich in London. Life on board the hulks was grim. Prisoners were stripped of all their possessions, dressed in shabby, ill-fitting clothes and placed in irons. Their living quarters were damp, dirty cells.

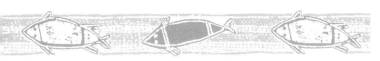

A period of planning followed, under the guidance of Lord Sydney, the Home Secretary. Arthur Phillip, a navy captain who had experience of transporting African slaves, was chosen to command the convict fleet. Marines led by Major Robert Ross were to accompany him and set up a garrison. But at this stage, no one knew whether Phillip's expedition would be the only convict voyage to Botany Bay or the first of many. The British had been to this distant region only once, in 1770. It was impossible to know what the future there would hold.

TERRA NULLIUS

The Beauchamp Committee asked Joseph Banks if he thought that the government should buy land for the new colony from the Aborigines. Banks replied that, as Aborigines were nomadic, they felt no attachment to territory. This was quite wrong, but it led Britain to claim that New South Wales was *terra nullius*, unoccupied land that it could use exactly as it pleased.

Captain Arthur Phillip

The British government hoped to build friendly relations with the Aborigines, as this extract from Arthur Phillip's commission shows. It was issued by King George III on 23 April 1787.

To open an intercourse with means 'to begin communication with'.

You are to endeavour by every possible means to open an intercourse with the natives... enjoining all our subjects to live in amity and kindness with them. And if any of our subjects shall...destroy them, or give them any unnecessary interruption in the exercise of their several occupations, it is our will and pleasure that you do cause such offenders to be brought to punishment according to the degree of the offence.

Amity means 'friendship'.

News of the proposed Botany Bay settlement spread fast. This is an extract from a song about the colony published in December 1786.

Let us drink a good health to our schemers above,
Who at length have contrived from this land to remove
Thieves, robbers and villains, they'll send 'em away,
To become a new people at Botany Bay.
...
The hulks and the jails had some thousands in store,
But out of the jails are ten thousand times more,
Who live by fraud, cheating, vile tricks and foul play,
They should all be sent over to Botany Bay.

ARRIVAL AND SETTLEMENT

THE FIRST FLEET

Captain Phillip's expedition, soon to become known as the First Fleet, finally left Portsmouth on 13 May 1787. The fleet consisted of 11 vessels and was led by the flagship *Sirius*, on which Phillip himself sailed. In all, about 1500 people set out on the journey – the captain and his nine staff, over 200 marines, some with their wives and children, about 400 sailors – and approximately 750 convicts (see pages 20-1).

The convicts were kept below decks on the transport ships. Their quarters were dark and cramped – a man of average height could not stand upright. Male criminals were chained, but women were put in irons only as a punishment. Seasickness was common and typhus hit the ships even before they sailed. But Captain Phillip and his surgeon, John White, did their best to keep convicts and crew healthy. The basic diet consisted of water, hardtack (a type of tough cracker), bread, salt pork

and beef, peas, oatmeal and cheese, but fruit and vegetables were added whenever possible to prevent scurvy. Air pipes, a new invention, were installed to improve ventilation, but often the atmosphere below decks was foul-smelling and stifling.

For reasons of wind and weather, the fleet did not take a direct route. It called first at Tenerife, one of the Canary Islands, then at Rio de Janeiro in Brazil, where cotton, coffee, orange, banana and many other plants were purchased for use in the new colony. Next, the ships doubled back across the Atlantic Ocean to the Cape of Good Hope in South Africa. There they took on board not only more plants but also hundreds of animals, including sheep, cattle and chickens.

The fleet left Africa on 13 November 1787 and reached Botany Bay between 18 and 20 January 1788. The site was a disappointment. The fertile soil and fresh water promised by Joseph Banks

THE ROUTE OF THE FIRST FLEET

Portsmouth, England
EUROPE
ASIA
N
Tenerife, Canary Islands
AFRICA
Pacific Ocean
SOUTH AMERICA
Rio de Janeiro, Brazil
Atlantic Ocean
Indian Ocean
AUSTRALIA
Botany Bay
Cape Town, South Africa
Van Diemen's Land

→ Portsmouth to Rio de Janeiro, 9800 km
→ Rio de Janeiro to Cape Town, 5300 km
→ Cape Town to Botany Bay, 10,500 km

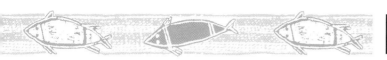
were nowhere to be seen. So, on 21 January, Captain Phillip and some of his crew sailed north in search of a better location. They found a beautiful harbour that Phillip named Sydney, after the British Home Secretary.

This painting of the arrival of the First Fleet in Botany Bay was made by William Bradley, the first lieutenant of the *Sirius*.

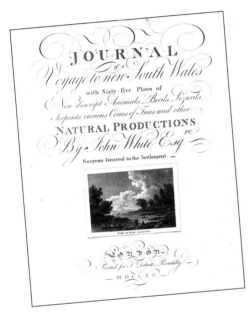

The elaborate title page of John White's book

At this point, the fleet was sailing from Tenerife to Rio.

The men here means 'the crew'.

Convicts often arrived from jail in rags.

The **boatswain** is the officer responsible for making sure that a ship and its equipment are in good working order.

The First Fleet surgeon, John White, wrote about his experiences in *Journal of a Voyage to New South Wales* (1790). The first extract shows his professional concern for the people on board the *Charlotte*, one of the transport ships. The second demonstrates his interest in natural history, which grew once he reached the new colony and discovered its many unique plants and animals.

The weather became exceedingly dark, warm, and close, with heavy rain, a temperature of the atmosphere very common on approaching the equator, and very much to be dreaded, as the health is greatly endangered thereby. Every attention was therefore paid to the people on board the Charlotte, and every exertion used to keep her clean and wholesome below decks. My first care was to keep the men... out of the rain; and I never suffered the convicts to come upon deck when it rained, as they had neither linen nor clothing sufficient to make themselves dry and comfortable after getting wet...

The boatswain struck... a most beautiful fish, about ten pounds weight. In shape it a good deal resembled a salmon, with this difference, that its tail was more forked. It was in colour of a lovely yellow; and when first taken out of the water, it had two beautiful stripes of green on each side, which some minutes after, changed to a delightful blue... The sailors gave it the name of the Yellow Tail.

CONVICTS

These two convicts were painted in Australia in 1793. Male and female convicts often lived as couples, but many men had no partner because of the shortage of women in the colony.

Although 778 convicts were loaded on to the First Fleet ships only about 736 actually sailed for Australia. The great majority – about 600 – were men. The average age of all the criminals was 27, although the age range ran from nine to 82. Some of the female convicts took their babies and young children with them.

The convicts had committed a variety of crimes, but most were thieves. Many, such as highwaymen, had used violence or the threat of violence. Many were also repeat offenders, whose law-breaking had not been curbed by earlier punishments. About 80 of the criminals were mutineers who had escaped from ships bound for America when it was the main destination for

A scene in London's Central Criminal Court, popularly known as the Old Bailey. This was where Tamasin Allen (see page 21) was tried.

convicts. None was a murderer and none a political prisoner, although later ships carried many of these types of criminal (see pages 36-7).

Despite the variety of crimes, the length of the transportation sentence handed down by the courts was usually a standard seven or 14 years. Most of the First Fleet convicts were serving seven-year sentences and many had already completed one or more years before they set out for New South Wales. They were soon to become free men and women – stranded far from their homes.

The convicts came from many parts of England, but London provided over one third of the First Fleet's convict cargo. The transport ships also carried a small number of Irish people. A large number of the convicts were poor and uneducated – only about half of the men and

a quarter of the women could write. About 12 per cent of the men were jobless, while others were everything from rural labourers to chimney sweeps. The women's occupations included laundry maid, milliner and dressmaker.

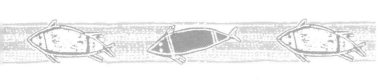

When reading the facts and statistics about the First Fleet convicts, it is easy to forget that each criminal had a more personal story, too. The documents shown here reveal exactly what some of them did to earn their sentences.

At that time, the pound was divided into twelve shillings. Each shilling contained 12 pence (d.). Five shillings a day was a good wage.

Peruke means 'wig'.

Name: Henry Abrams
Age: 26
Place of Trial: Chelmsford, Essex
The court report charged Abrams with three offences of highway robbery. During the first he was said to have stolen the following:
'one linen Ruffled Shirt of the value of **five shillings** one Muslin Neckcloth of the value of 12d. one pair of Men's Leather Breeches of the value of 10 shillings one Man's **Peruke** of the value of 2 shillings one stuff Bag of the value of 2 shillings and one pair of Leather Boot Garters of the value of 12d. one Piece of Gold Coin...called a half Guinea...and fifteen shillings in monies numbered.'
Sentence: 7 years' transportation.

The chapel of Magdalen College, Oxford, where Thomas Gearing (below) committed his crime, can be seen in the background of this painting.

Name: Tamasin Allen
Age: 32
Place of Trial: Old Bailey, London
The court report explained Allen's crime as follows:
'Tamasin Allen... was indicted for... assaulting Hugh Harding... and putting him in... fear and danger of his life, and... taking from his person... one leather pocket-book... ten grains of rose diamonds... seven grains weight of other diamonds... two brilliant diamonds... a pearl... one topaz... a silver pencil-case and one... bank note, value 10l.'
Sentence: 7 years' transportation.

l. means 'pound'.

An **Offertory Plate** is a large plate in which worshippers place their offerings of money during the collection in a church service.

Name: Thomas Gearing
Age: 42
Place of Trial: Oxford
The court report explained Gearing's crime, which he carried out with others, as follows:
'Last Saturday, between One and Two o'Clock in the Morning...the Chapel of Magdalen College, in this University, was robbed of two Pair of... Candlesticks, one Pair of which was Silver, and a **large Silver Offertory Plate**. The Villains who committed this Robbery had found Means to enter the College by a Ladder, into the Wood Yard at the Foot of Magdalen Bridge; from whence, through the Kitchen and Cloysters, they got to the Chapel, which they opened by a false key.'
Sentence: Transportation for life

COLONY-BUILDING

As soon as Captain Phillip had chosen the site of the new settlement (see page 19), he returned to Botany Bay and announced his decision. At once the fleet began preparations for the 16-kilometre journey north. Phillip, together with a group of officers and marines, was back in Sydney by 26 January. On the evening of that day, the Union Jack flag was raised on the shore. This event is still commemorated in Australia every year on Australia Day.

The next morning the male convicts began to arrive. They cleared the ground, which was covered with eucalyptus trees. They put up tents and Captain Phillip's wood-framed, canvas house. They unloaded stores and

animals, and sowed vegetable seeds and corn. On 6 February the female convicts disembarked. A day later the community assembled, the marine band played and King George III's commission, which made Phillip the colony's governor and outlined his duties, was read aloud to everyone.

Once the colony was established, the heavy work continued under the blazing sun (Australia's summer runs from December to February). Wooden huts, a storehouse and a hospital were all built, as well as Government House, a new, brick residence for the governor. A permanent church opened in August 1793, thanks to the efforts of the colony chaplain,

Reverend Richard Johnson. A court system was also set up, headed by the Judge-Advocate of New South Wales, David Collins.

Gradually, the colony spread. On 14 February 1788, the governor sent the *Supply* to Norfolk Island. On board were Lieutenant Philip Gidley King, various officials and 15 convicts. Their task was to cultivate the island's timber and flax, in the hope that they could be used for shipbuilding and sail-making. In November, a new mainland settlement was set up at

The momentous raising of the Union Jack flag in Sydney on 26 January 1788, as depicted by a 19th-century artist. Captain Arthur Phillip and the other naval officers are dressed in blue. The men in red are marines.

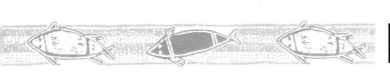
Parramatta, west of Sydney, where the soil was more fertile. Toongabbie, another site nearby, was soon settled, too.

The settlers' work almost came to nothing. The first harvest failed, so food had to be strictly rationed. Soon people began to starve. In desperation, Governor Phillip sent the *Sirius* to China for supplies, but it was wrecked off Norfolk Island. All seemed lost until, in June 1790, the Second Fleet arrived with food – and more convicts. The Third Fleet reached New South Wales the next year. The colony had become a regular part of the British penal system.

Judge-Advocate David Collins' two-volume book, *An Account of the English Colony in New South Wales* (1798/1802), provides a thorough and accurate account of the settlement's early days. The first extract below describes the arrival of the male convicts at Sydney. The second describes the foundation of the Parramatta site.

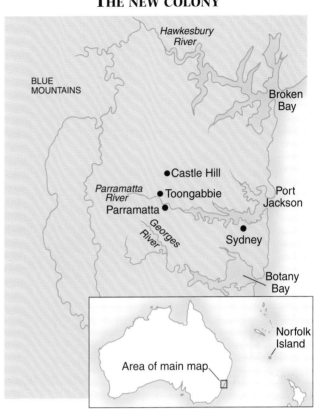

THE NEW COLONY

The disembarkation of the troops and convicts took place from the following day [27 January]... Parties of people were everywhere heard and seen variously employed; some in clearing ground for the... encampments; others in pitching tents, or bringing up... stores; and the spot which had so lately been the abode of silence and tranquillity was now changed to that of noise, clamour and confusion...

The month of November commenced with the establishment of the new settlement. On the 2d, His Excellency the Governor went to... choose the spot... Ten convicts who understood the business of cultivation were ordered to clear some land on a rising ground, which His Excellency named Rose Hill. The soil at this spot was of a stiff clayey nature, free from that rock which every where covered the surface at Sydney Cove, well clothed with timber and unobstructed by underwood.

Governor Phillip chose the name **Rose Hill** but, from 1791, the area was known by its Aboriginal name, Parramatta, meaning 'place of eels'.

CONVICT LIFE

Once they arrived in New South Wales, all convicts had to work for the government until their sentences expired. Gradually, a two-tier labour system developed. A minority of convicts was directly employed by the governor and his officials. The rest were 'assigned' to freed convicts and free settlers, and worked for their businesses.

In the early days of settlement, all male convicts carried out public works such as building. But eventually only about ten per cent were employed in government service. These convicts hacked roads through mountains, constructed bridges and barracks, and cultivated crops on public farms. The working day lasted for ten hours during the week and for six hours on Saturdays. The men were usually free to hire out their labour for money once the day's government work was over.

The assignment system – the government allocation of convicts to other employers – was first properly organised in New South Wales by Lieutenant Philip Gidley King when he became governor in 1800. Assigned men worked the same unpaid hours as those in government service and had the same right to earn money outside those hours. Their employers had to feed, house and clothe them. As a result, the government saved a great deal of money. By scattering convicts throughout the colony, assignment also reduced the risk of rebellion.

Many female convicts were assigned in the same way as the men. Those who remained in government service were often set to work in hospitals or orphanages. Others were sent to the Female Factory at Parramatta, which was set up by Governor King in 1804 and rebuilt in 1821. There, in filthy conditions, the women spun wool, wove fabric and ran a busy laundry. Some women, penniless and far from home, sank into prostitution and were readily exploited by both convicts and marines.

There was a third way for convicts who had not yet received their pardon (see pages 26-7). They could obtain tickets-of-leave. These precious documents, often granted for good conduct, permitted their owners to work entirely for wages in any job that they chose. But they were valid for only twelve months at a time and could be withdrawn by the government for various offences, including laziness.

A group of convicts in leg irons. Some of the convicts are wearing trousers with buttons down the side. This made it possible for them to undress without taking off their irons.

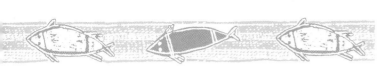
SECONDARY PUNISHMENT

Many convicts who committed further crimes after arriving in New South Wales were sent for secondary punishment in special penal settlements. These included Macquarie Harbour in Van Diemen's Land, Moreton Bay in present-day Queensland, and Norfolk Island. The most notorious of them all was Port Arthur, which was set up on a remote Van Diemen's Land peninsula in 1830. The treatment of convicts in these settlements was brutal. Men were chained, beaten and forced to carry out long hours of back-breaking labour.

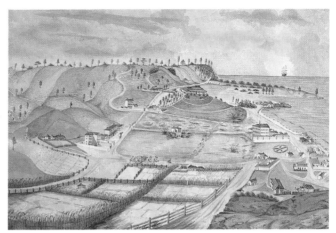

This painting shows the earliest settlement on Norfolk Island.

Convicts had to complete a fixed work task every day or week. This list, adapted from *Established General Orders, and Colonial Regulations*, published in Sydney in 1808, shows what was expected of them.

A **rod** is a unit of area equal to 25 square metres.

One **acre** is equal to 0.4 of a hectare.

Falling forest timber
Burning off timber
Breaking up new ground
Breaking up rubble
Reaping
Holing and planting corn
Splitting **6 feet paling**

WEEK'S WORK
1 acre 1 man
65 rods 1 man
65 rods 1 man
130 rods 1 man
1 acre 60 rods 1 man
1½ acre 1 man
2500 3 men

Six feet is equal to 1.8 metres.
Paling means 'wooden fence posts'.

Some convicts who re-offended were put in chain gangs and sent to build roads. The labour was exhausting – the men had to break up solid rock with pickaxes and shovels, then drag the rubble away in carts. In this extract, taken from *Recollections of Life in Van Diemen's Land*, Canadian convict William Gates tells of his road gang experiences.

Gang **overseers** were often convicts themselves but did not hesitate to punish their fellow criminals harshly, for example by flogging.

So long as we could crawl about, or could lift a finger, we were brutally compelled to the task. The fourth day the overseer began to lay the work to us in earnest. He was anxious to hold his petty situation, and therefore strove to please his superior tyrants... Though a number of our gang were really too unwell to labor... they chose to follow us to the roads, rather than to stay alone in the miserable huts, that always swarmed with fleas and lice...

EMANCIPISTS

Most convicts gained their freedom only after they had completed their sentences. However, some were granted pardons and they became known as Emancipists. The word was also used to describe ex-convicts whose sentences had expired, although the correct term for them was 'expirees'.

The government granted conditional pardons for various reasons, including good conduct. Convicts who arrived with specialist skills, for example as printers, were often pardoned, too. In this way they became free to use their abilities for the benefit of the colony. People with conditional pardons were 'free on the ground', that is free in New South Wales but not allowed to return home. Absolute pardons were usually granted only when a convict was found to have suffered a wrongful conviction. Such convicts were free to go home – but they had to find their own fare.

Up to about 1820, many Emancipists were given grants of land in the hope that they would grow crops and no longer need food from the public stores. The first Emancipist farmer to make his mark was James Ruse, an expiree. His plot in Parramatta, known as Experiment Farm, flourished for some years. But after he moved to the Hawkesbury River in 1794 he began to drink his

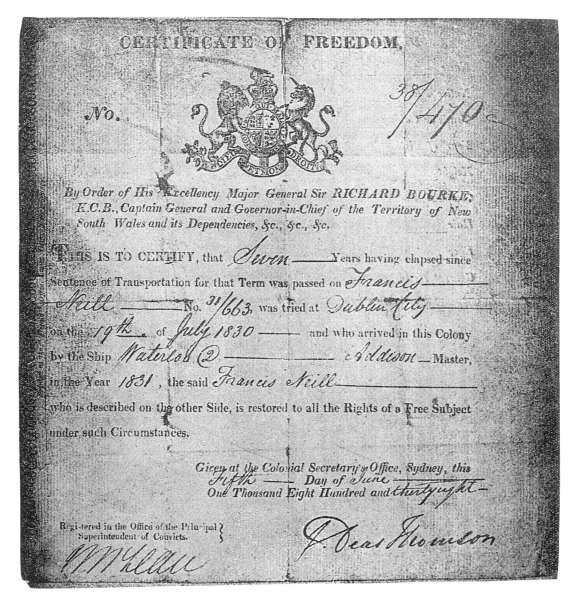

This Certificate of Freedom was issued to convict Francis Mill in 1838, at the end of his seven-year sentence. Mill stood trial in Dublin, Ireland.

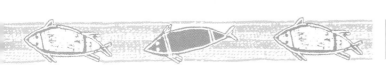
money away, and he ended his life working on another man's land. This pattern of gain then loss was common.

Many Emancipists contributed to the life of the colony in other ways. Francis Greenway, a professional architect turned forger, designed many of Sydney's finest public buildings (see page 33). James Underwood and Henry Kable became the most successful shipbuilders in New South Wales, while Simeon Lord was a merchant who dealt in everything from whale meat to wood. William Redfern was the colony's leading doctor. One-time horse stealer Mary Haydock expanded the shipping and other businesses of her husband Thomas Reibey after he died and became very rich.

The Emancipists' position in society was awkward. Some free settlers, known as the Exclusives, thought that the Emancipists should never enjoy the same rights as people who had not committed crimes. In contrast, one governor, Lachlan Macquarie (see pages 32-3), and the politician and explorer William Charles Wentworth, fought tirelessly for their cause. The dispute rumbled on until the end of the convict era – and beyond.

Mary Reibey was an Emancipist whose husband died when she was in her mid-30s. After his death, she successfully managed her complex business interests.

THE NAME GAME

Emancipists did not like to be reminded of their convict origins so they often said that they had been 'government men'. The wealthiest Exclusives were also known by another name – pure merinos. This referred to the type of pedigree sheep that they owned, which had never mixed with other breeds.

In a speech made in 1821, Governor Macquarie described how he thought New South Wales should treat Emancipists.

'[This colony] should be made the home AND A HAPPY HOME to every emancipated convict who DESERVES IT... My principle is, that when once a man is free, his former state should no longer be remembered, or allowed to act against him; let him then feel himself eligible for any situation which he has, by a long term of upright conduct, proved himself worthy of filling.'

This simple but touching poem was carved on the gravestone of the Emancipist farmer James Ruse.

My Mother Reread Me Tenderley
With me She Took Much Paines
And when I arived in This Coelney
I sowd the Forst Grain and Now
With My Hevenly Father I hope
For Ever To Remain.

Reread is a misspelling for 'reared'.

Coelney is a misspelling for 'colony'.

Forst is a misspelling for 'first'.

EUROPEANS AND ABORIGINES

When the First Fleet reached New South Wales, the Aborigines shouted "Go away!". But it was Captain Phillip's duty to establish good relations with the region's original inhabitants. So he offered them beads and other trinkets. In return the Aborigines helped Europeans to find water and fish. However, this happy pattern of exchange did not last for long.

Over the next few years, Phillip continued his attempts at friendship. He decided that it was essential for him to learn the local Aboriginal language. In 1789 he captured an Aborigine called Bennelong and took informal lessons from him. Bennelong escaped, but the men's relationship continued and each managed to grasp the basics of the other's language.

William Bradley (see page 19) painted this picture. It shows the white newcomers' first meeting with Aboriginal women, in 1788.

In 1792, when Phillip went back to England, Bennelong visited, too, and was presented to King George III.

The general situation between the two communities steadily worsened, however. Convicts began to steal Aboriginal weapons and tools. The Aborigines struck back by spearing and often killing the thieves. Conflict increased as European settlement expanded and Aboriginal tribes were forced off their lands. Soon guerrilla warfare erupted along the frontiers. A daring man called Pemulwuy led many raids by Botany Bay Aborigines until he was shot dead in 1802.

After Arthur Phillip left the colony, governors such as Philip Gidley King (see page 24) passed laws designed to protect both Aborigines and settlers. But murders of both blacks and whites increased. As the evidence of Aborigines was not accepted

A portrait of Bennelong painted in 1795

in court, their killers were rarely convicted. Governors also attempted to 'civilise' Aborigines by converting them to Christianity and sending them to school.

As Europeans continued to spread, Aboriginal resistance grew. About 20,000 Aborigines died in frontier clashes and brutal massacres. At least 28 were killed in the 1838 Myall Creek Massacre. However, some

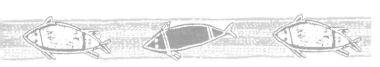

This 19th-century picture shows Aborigines setting fire to their territory in northern Australia in an attempt to drive white settlers away. This technique was quite commonly used.

Aborigines changed sides, joining the native police forces which protected white farms and homes. In the end, loss of land and food supplies, disease and guns combined to defeat the Aborigines. By 1888 their numbers had fallen to 50,000 and large parts of their ancient territories were in European hands.

The arrival of Europeans brought Aborigines into contact with several new diseases against which they had no immunity. Smallpox epidemics swept through their communities several times. Cholera, influenza and measles also killed many. In this dispatch dated 13 February 1790, Governor Phillip gives details of the smallpox outbreak that took place in 1789.

In the beginning of the following April numbers of the natives were found dead with the small-pox in different parts of the harbour... It is not possible to determine the number of natives who were carried off by this fatal disorder. It must be great; and judging from the information of the native now living with us... one-half of those who inhabit this part of the country died; and as the natives always retired from where the disorder appeared, and which some must have carried with them, it must have been spread to a considerable distance, as well inland as along the coast. We have seen the traces of it wherever we have been.

VAN DIEMEN'S LAND

The British colonised Van Diemen's Land in 1803 and soon clashes broke out between the local Aborigines and the sheep-farming settlers. In 1830, over 2000 men tried to capture all the Aborigines by sweeping across the island in a cordon known as the Black Line. They failed – only two were caught. However, an Englishman called George Augustus Robinson persuaded the Aborigines to leave. By 1834, they had all gone to Flinders Island in the Bass Strait. Most perished. The 47 survivors returned to Van Diemen's Land in 1846, but the last of them died 30 years later. Some Tasmanian Aborigines still live on nearby islands.

Truganini was said to be the last Aborigine in Van Diemen's Land (Tasmania). She died there in 1876.

THE NEW SOUTH WALES CORPS

The New South Wales Corps was a British army unit created in 1789 especially for service in the colony. Its first members – two companies, a total of 100 men – arrived on the Second Fleet in 1790. More followed in 1792. They soon began to play a vital role in colonial life.

The men of the New South Wales Corps had a wide variety of duties. In particular, they supervised convicts, especially those on government service and in places of secondary punishment. They also patrolled the frontiers of settlement and repelled Aboriginal attacks. Corps officers sat on the bench with the Judge-Advocate at some trials (see page 22) and helped him to decide on verdicts and types of sentences.

When Arthur Phillip retired in 1792, his post as governor was taken by the commander of the New South Wales Corps, Major Francis Grose. He increased the food rations of his men and gave them land – ordinary soldiers usually received 25 acres, officers 100 acres. He also replaced many important civilian officials with military men. In 1794, William Paterson, a Corps captain, succeeded Grose and followed similar policies.

Corps officers were allowed to borrow money by offering the regiment's wealth as security. As

John Macarthur came into conflict with several governors of New South Wales, including John Hunter, before the showdown with Bligh. His rebellious nature earned him the nickname 'the Perturbator'.

a result, they had funds to invest in money-making schemes. In 1792 a group of Corps officers jointly chartered a ship, the *Britannia*, to bring in supplies for them to sell at a profit. A year later, they bought rum from another ship, the *Hope*. Soon they had a monopoly on many goods including rum, which became a substitute currency.

The New South Wales Corps effectively ran the colony for some years. Then, in 1806, William Bligh became governor and limited the rum-trading. At the same time he clashed with John Macarthur, a rich landowner who had been the Corps paymaster. On 26 January 1808, Macarthur and Corps officers led by Major George

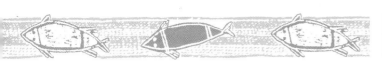

The arrest of Governor Bligh during the Rum Rebellion. In reality, he was probably hiding behind a bed rather than cowering underneath it.

Johnston began the so-called Rum Rebellion. Bligh was placed under arrest and returned to England in 1810. Johnston was court-martialled in 1811, found guilty and dismissed from the army. The Corps was replaced by the 73rd Regiment (see page 32).

THE CASTLE HILL
UPRISING

The New South Wales Corps suppressed the only major convict rebellion that took place on mainland Australia in the transportation era. In 1804, a group of Irish convicts seized the farming settlement of Castle Hill, north of Parramatta. Then they moved towards Sydney. The Corps was warned of their approach and met them at a place called Vinegar Hill. Major Johnston and his men easily defeated the rebels. Their two main leaders, William Johnston and Phillip Cunningham, were hanged, along with six more. Other participants were flogged.

Governor Bligh was a notorious character. In 1789, when he was captain of the ship HMS *Bounty*, his crew mutinied. In Sydney he made many more enemies, in particular by forcing people out of their homes so that he could rebuild parts of the city. But in his own mind he was a moral crusader, rescuing the citizens of Sydney from drink and decay. This is how he explained himself at Major Johnston's court-martial on 7 May 1811.

I arrived there on the 6th August [1806]... To ascertain the state of the colony, I visited many of the inhabitants... and witnessed many melancholy proofs of their wretched condition... Sydney, the head quarters, formed some exception... yet there the habitations and public storehouses were falling into decay; industry was declining, while a pernicious fondness for spirituous liquors was gaining ground, to the destruction of public morals and private happiness.

Pernicious means 'harmful'.

Spirituous liquors means 'alcohol'.

CHAPTER 3

MACQUARIE AND AFTER

GOVERNOR MACQUARIE

Lachlan Macquarie, a few years before he left for Australia

Sydney as it looked in 1821, the final year of Macquarie's governorship

Lieutenant-Colonel Lachlan Macquarie, a Scot who had many years of army service to his credit, became Governor of New South Wales in 1810. He faced a daunting task, as the colony was in some disarray after the Rum Rebellion against William Bligh (see pages 30-1). But Macquarie was a man of great strength and vision, and was ably supported by his wife, Elizabeth.

Macquarie made an immediate start. He replaced the colony's judge and many other officials with his own hand-picked men. At the same time he created several new posts, including that of Colonial Secretary. Macquarie did not punish the men of the former New South Wales Corps for their part in the anti-Bligh rebellion. Some joined the 73rd Regiment, which arrived with Macquarie and afterwards provided the colony's main military strength.

Macquarie then aimed at wider reforms. He promoted Christian morality by encouraging people to marry rather than live together. He made church attendance compulsory for convicts and continued the crackdown on rum. He also introduced a programme of public works such

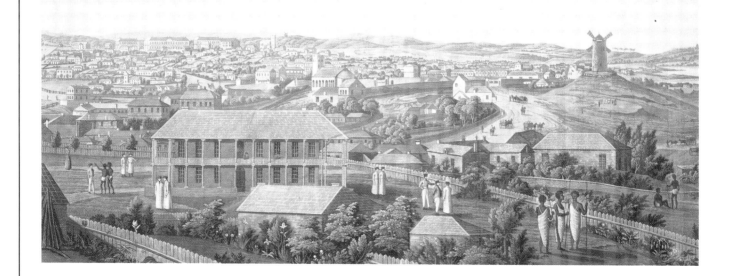

St James's Church in Sydney was built with bricks made by convicts.

AUSTRALIA

The explorer Matthew Flinders (see page 41) first suggested replacing the name 'New Holland' with 'Australia' in a book published in 1814. Three years later, Macquarie wrote to the British government recommending the name 'Australia'. So he was responsible for the continent's present-day name, which was also carved on his tombstone.

as road construction, which used convict labour. His most visible project was the transformation of Sydney from a shabby town into a city. In 1816, Macquarie made the convict Francis Greenway government architect. By 1822, Greenway had designed more than 40 buildings, including Hyde Park Barracks and St James's Church.

Macquarie wanted New South Wales to offer Emancipists as well as free settlers the opportunity for success (see pages 26-7). He also wanted to prepare convicts for a better life, rather than simply to punish them. Macquarie treated Aborigines with respect, too, although he tried to turn them into settled farmers and introduced many harsh regulations in an effort to stop frontier clashes.

Macquarie's leniency led to his downfall. The Exclusives (see pages 26-7) plotted against him, while the British government believed that his fair treatment of convicts was making transportation less of a deterrent. The government also became alarmed at the cost of the colony's public works. A judge, John Bigge, was sent to review the situation and, in 1821, Macquarie resigned. The Bigge reports criticised him, supported the Exclusives, and set up a New South Wales legislative council. No future governor ever had as much power as Macquarie.

Hyde Park Barracks was built to house convicts. This is how Governor Macquarie described part of its 1819 opening ceremony in his diary.

I went to the Convict Barrack... to see the Convicts sit down to their first Dinner... This was a most highly gratifying and interesting sight; no less than 580 Convicts having sat down to a most excellent Dinner; Plum Pudding and an allowance of Punch being allowed to them, in addition to their regular Meal on this auspicious Day. – I addressed them in a short plain speech... Mrs. M. and myself, and the Friends who accompanied us, drank to their Health & Prosperity. They all appeared very happy and Contented, and gave us three Cheers on our coming away.

FREE SETTLERS

In the early years of New South Wales, few free settlers (non-convicts) went to the colony. By 1828, there were fewer than 5000 free settlers in a total population of over 36,000. However, the growing attractions of Australia and problems in Great Britain and Ireland soon began to alter this balance.

The first free immigrants to Australia had to pay their own way, so most were reasonably wealthy people who hoped to make a greater fortune overseas. They were drawn by the promise of grants of free land from colonial governments eager to attract respectable citizens. In addition, they could depend on free convict labour, which was readily available thanks to the convict assignment system (see page 24).

Events in Britain soon led to a broader range of people becoming free settlers. The Agricultural and Industrial revolutions (see page 12) left thousands unemployed. Many of those in work received low pay and lived in slum conditions. In Scotland, the Highland Clearances saw many landowners turning their crofters (farmers) out of their farms and off their land. In Ireland, the potato famine in the late 1840s led to widespread starvation and misery. Meanwhile in Australia, farmers and pastoralists (see pages 38-9) were desperate for labourers. The solution was for the jobless to go to the jobs.

Unfortunately, most of the unemployed could not afford to travel. The answer to this problem was assisted migration,

Edward Gibbon Wakefield had many theories about how Australia should be run – despite the fact that he never actually went to the colony.

first suggested by the English political theorist Edward Gibbon Wakefield. He proposed that Australian land should be sold instead of being given away. The money raised would then be used to pay for poor immigrants' fares. This scheme began in 1831. Another scheme, the bounty system, was introduced in 1835. Its aim was to increase the number of skilled immigrants. They were chosen at a distance by Australian employers who received money for each new arrival. In practice, however, selection was left to shipping agents in Britain who simply packed their ships and pocketed the money.

Between 1788 and 1850, about 187,000 free settlers went to Australia. Not all were would-be landowners and labourers. Some professionals, such as doctors and lawyers, made their

This romantic, mid-19th century picture shows a family of free settlers newly arrived in Australia. The sheep and fruit suggest that a life of farming lies ahead.

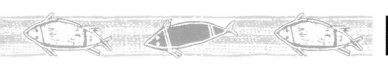

way there, as well as military officers who found themselves redundant at the end of the Napoleonic Wars (see page 36). Not all went to New South Wales. From the beginning of the 19th century, several more colonies were founded and settled (see pages 42-3).

(see page 36)
(see pages 42-3)

THE SEA PASSAGE

By the 1830s, the sea voyage to Australia still took over three months. During that time, rich passengers lived in cabins and were free to walk about on deck. The poor were confined to steerage, below decks, where conditions were often worse than those endured by convicts. There was a danger of shipwreck, too. Most vessels no longer called at South Africa on the way to Australia, but sailed further south, near Antarctica. There, vast waves and icebergs claimed hundreds of lives.

Englishwoman Caroline Chisholm went to Australia with her husband in 1838. She became concerned at the plight of immigrant women, who often had nowhere to go and ended up sleeping rough. She set up a women's hostel in Sydney, then met every ship and took new arrivals there. Chisholm also helped other immigrants to find homes and jobs.

After returning to England in 1846, Chisholm encouraged the government to provide more funds for emigration. In 1850, she set up the Family Colonisation Loan Society, which lent poor families their fares to Australia. This extract comes from Chisholm's *Emigration and Transportation Relatively Considered* (1847).

Caroline Chisholm's work with immigrants was largely inspired by her Roman Catholic faith.

Port Phillip was the name originally given to the present-day Australian state of Victoria.

> 5
>
> first year, (allowing four months for the passage,) would amount to.............................£17,400
> and for the remaining three years to 78,300
> ————
> Total receipts in 4 years........£95,700
>
> The number which I have named, my Lord, must not be considered as the total number our Australian Colonies could provide for, as it is merely intended to show the economy of emigration even on a small scale. The demand for labour in New South Wales, Port Phillip, and South Australia, is urgent and increasing. Is it not a lamentable thought, then, my Lord, that deaths should daily result from starvation among British subjects, while in this valuable colony good wheat is rotting on the ground for the want of hands to gather it in;—that tens of thousands of fine sheep, droves after droves, thousands upon thousands of fat cattle are annually slaughtered there and "*boiled down,*" in order to be rendered into tallow for the European market, while the vast refuse is cast into the fields to be devoured by dogs and pigs, and yet no effort is made by England to provide for her struggling people by a humane system of colonization. Let me then, in the name of suffering humanity, entreat of your Lordship to take into mature and immediate consideration, this demand for labour—this fearful waste of human food, and withal the vast capabilities of our Australasian Colonies, (nearly equal in size to all Europe); and let me hope that the result of your Lordship's deliberation, and that of other friends of humanity, will be to give to some of our starving peasantry a passage

The demand for labour in New South Wales, **Port Phillip**, and South Australia, is urgent and increasing. Is it not a lamentable thought, then... that deaths should daily result from starvation among British subjects, while in this valuable colony good wheat is rotting on the ground for the want of hands to gather it in; – that tens of thousands of fine sheep, droves after droves, thousands upon thousands of fat cattle are annually slaughtered... while the vast refuse is cast into the fields to be devoured by dogs and pigs, and yet no effort is made by England to provide for her struggling people by a humane system of colonization.

GROWTH AND CHANGE

A fierce-looking member of the Metropolitan Police questions a young boy. The uniform of the new force was blue to make it clearly distinguishable from the red uniform of soldiers.

A large group of convicts awaits transportation at Chatham Dockyard, Kent, in 1828.

After 1815, convict numbers soared. In that year, 1074 transportees went to Australia. In 1816 about 2600 reached the continent, and in 1835 almost 5000. There were many reasons for this dramatic rise.

The Napoleonic Wars, in which Britain and its allies fought France, came to an end in 1815. As a result, thousands of soldiers and sailors became unemployed. Many turned to crime. The establishment of London's Metropolitan Police Force by Robert Peel in 1829 meant that far more criminals were caught than ever before. In addition, new British laws made transportation the punishment for large numbers of offences that had once carried the death penalty. These three factors all contributed greatly to the increase in numbers of convicts.

Continuing unrest in Ireland led to a rise in the number of political prisoners. A few Irish convicts left Britain on the First Fleet. Soon after, transports began to sail from Ireland itself and often carried men and women whose only crime was to resist British rule. Over 200 were packed off to Australia after the Irish rebellion of 1798, and many of the same people took part in the Castle Hill Uprising (see page 31). Violence in Ireland increased during the 19th century, as its inhabitants fought against greedy landowners and against the British government. These activists swelled convict numbers, too.

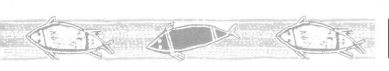

Political disturbances in England also added to the convict boom. Many Luddites and Swing rioters (see page 14) ended up in Australia. The Tolpuddle Martyrs (see above) were transported in 1834. However, they received an absolute pardon two years later. Some Chartists, who from 1838 to 1848 fought for political reforms in Britain, also sailed out on the transport ships.

This great wave of convicts endured harsh new regimes in New South Wales and in Van Diemen's Land which, from 1825, was ruled separately. As Governor of New South Wales (1825-31), Sir Ralph Darling ended the leniency of the Macquarie era (see pages 32-3). The flogging of convicts became much more common under his rule, and remained so. From

Four of the six Tolpuddle Martyrs. These farm labourers came from the Dorset village of Tolpuddle. They were convicted for organising trade union activities, but they quickly became popular heroes.

1833 to 1836, a quarter of male convicts was severely flogged each year. In Van Diemen's Land, Colonel George Arthur set up the much-feared penal settlement of Port Arthur (see page 25).

In 1834, a prison was established for the growing number of boy convicts aged nine to 18. The prison was called Point Puer (*puer* is Latin for 'boy') and was located near Port Arthur in Van Diemen's Land. At its height, it had 730 inmates. In this extract, the commandant officer of Port Arthur, Charles O'Hara Booth, explains how the boys live.

Viz. means 'that is'.

Bed-tick means 'mattress'.

Who conduct themselves means 'who behave well'.

The Juvenile establishment at Point Puer was formed in January 1834... The whole of the boys are more or less taught the use of husbandry – tools, the axe, saw, etc... The clothing furnished to the boys is the same as that allowed to other prisoners throughout the colony; viz. two jackets, two pairs of trousers, two pairs of boots, two striped cotton shirts, one cloth waistcoat, and a cap, annually. The bedding consists of one rug, one blanket, one bed-tick or hammock. As the barrack room is rather cold, I have taken it upon myself to issue an extra blanket to the boys who conduct themselves, but which is taken from them when sleeping in the cells, etc., or under punishment.

PASTORALISTS AND FARMERS

Elizabeth Macarthur, wife of the pastoralist John Macarthur. During her husband's frequent absences, Elizabeth ran their sheep farm very successfully, increasing their landholdings to 60,000 acres (more than 24,000 hectares).

Crop-growing was essential for the survival of Australia's first settlers. Farms gradually spread and the newcomers learned to deal with the colony's soil and vegetation, as well as its floods and droughts. Animals were also raised, but it was not until explorers crossed the Blue Mountains that pastoralists and graziers (sheep and cattle farmers) began to flourish.

The most important early pastoralist was John Macarthur (see pages 30-1). In 1793, he set up a sheep farm in Parramatta, which he named after his wife, Elizabeth. While in England in 1801, Macarthur showed wool from the sheep to Lord Camden, a high-ranking politician. Camden urged Macarthur to produce wool for British markets and arranged for him to be granted 5000 acres of New South Wales land. On his return, Macarthur cross-bred his sheep with imported Spanish merinos to create a new, strong breed with a good fleece.

The first three Europeans to cross the Blue Mountains, west of Sydney, were Gregory Blaxland, William Lawson and William Charles Wentworth (see pages 40-1). Their expedition took place in 1813, and a year later convicts began to build a road across the mountains. Once it was complete, in 1815, vast new expanses of good grazing land were open to settlers. Governor Ralph Darling (see

Drovers urge their cattle across a river on the way to market.

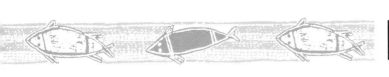
page 37) tried to limit settlement to the 19 counties that he established in 1829. But men and women eager for land crossed the boundaries of these counties without a thought. These people were known as squatters.

The squatters took over large areas of land for their sheep and cattle farms, called runs. In 1836, they were given the right to graze animals on payment of a licence fee. In 1847, they gained security of tenure (the legal right to remain on the land). Soon they controlled almost all the best land. Conflict followed after the 1850s, as new settlers demanded the right to select ground for crop farms. Colonial governments passed laws allowing these selectors to set up small farms. However, poor land and unsuitable farming methods caused many of these new farms to fail.

THE WOOL INDUSTRY

The Australian wool industry began to flourish in the 1830s and wool quickly became the country's most valuable export. At fixed times each year sheep were shorn, herded to and from markets, and slaughtered. As the 19th century progressed, methods changed. Wire was used to fence sheep in, and machines speeded up shearing. In the 1890s, depression hit the industry because of over-expansion and falling wool prices. However by the early 20th century, it was thriving again.

A sheep drover and his dog keep their flock under control.

Alexander Harris went to New South Wales as a free settler in 1825. His book *Settlers and Convicts* (1847) tells of his life there, including the period that he spent on a sheep run. Experts think that Harris sometimes mingled fiction with fact, but that the book provides a largely accurate picture. In the first extract, he gives details of the opossum cloaks often worn by shepherds. In the second, he describes a shepherd's hut.

Blacks here means 'Aborigines'.

1 inch is equal to 2.5cm.
1 foot is equal to 30.5cm.

An opossum's skin is about as large as that of a cat, and when stretched out and dried, cuts to about 15 inches by 8 or 10. Thus dried, and with all the hair on, the blacks sew them together to the number of from 30 to 60; white men also have learned the art; so manufactured they make a capital protection from the weather, either by day or night.

This hut was one large apartment, and had ground for the floor: at one end was the fire-place... at the other the shepherds used to sleep, spreading their beds on sheets of bark just lifted off the ground by having logs of wood about 8 inches thick and 3 feet long laid underneath, one at the head, the other at the feet...

ACROSS AUSTRALIA

Almost as soon as the First Fleet arrived, people began to explore the vast spaces of Australia.

The first important expedition took place in 1813, when Blaxland, Lawson and Wentworth crossed the Blue Mountains (see page 38). Charles Sturt led the next major journeys. In 1828, he discovered the Darling River. In 1829, he explored the Murrumbidgee River, then continued into the Murray River and followed it down to the sea.

Edward John Eyre led several expeditions from the Adelaide area. His aim was to find the inland sea mistakenly believed to lie at the heart of the continent. In 1839, Eyre reached the

peninsula later named after him, and the Flinders Range. In 1840 he sailed to Albany, then trekked to Perth on the west coast. Later in 1840, he tried to head north from Adelaide. This proved impossible, so he went west, became the first European to cross the Nullarbor Plain, and reached Albany once more.

In 1844, Sturt took over the search for the inland sea. He too set out from Adelaide, but managed to make his way much further north, to the Simpson Desert. However, the blistering heat and lack of water forced him to end the expedition.

At the same time, Prussian explorer Ludwig Leichhardt was heading in a different direction. In

1844, he set out from Moreton Bay and the following year reached Port Essington, at Australia's northern tip. In 1846, he tried to make an east-west crossing of the continent, but failed. During his second attempt, in 1848, Leichhardt disappeared.

Robert O'Hara Burke and William John Wills set out to cross Australia from south to north. The expedition left Melbourne in 1860 and established camps at Menindie and Cooper's Creek on the route. Only Burke, Wills, Charles Gray and John King made the final trek north, reaching their goal in 1861. Gray died on the way back to Cooper's Creek. When the other three got there, they

THE EUROPEAN EXPLORATION OF AUSTRALIA

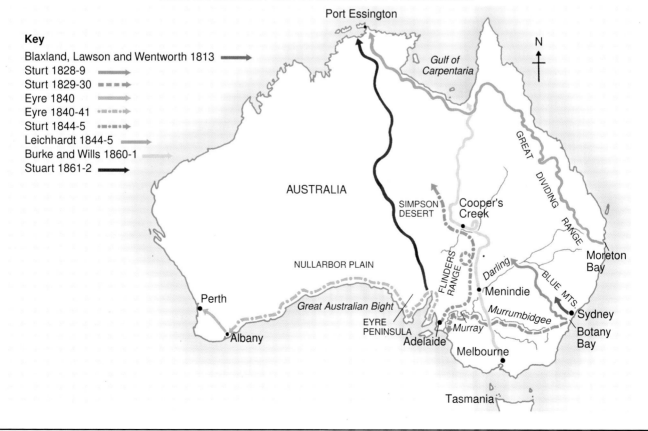

Key
Blaxland, Lawson and Wentworth 1813
Sturt 1828-9
Sturt 1829-30
Eyre 1840
Eyre 1840-41
Sturt 1844-5
Leichhardt 1844-5
Burke and Wills 1860-1
Stuart 1861-2

Port Essington
Gulf of Carpentaria
N
AUSTRALIA
GREAT DIVIDING RANGE
SIMPSON DESERT
Cooper's Creek
NULLARBOR PLAIN
FLINDERS RANGE
Darling
Moreton Bay
Perth
Great Australian Bight
EYRE PENINSULA
Menindie
BLUE MTS
Murrumbidgee
Sydney
Albany
Murray
Botany Bay
Adelaide
Melbourne
Tasmania

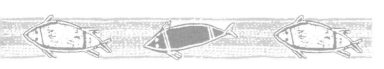

The Burke and Wills expedition sets out from Melbourne amid great excitement and cheering.

SHORE SURVEYS

Before expeditions into Australia's interior began, Englishmen Matthew Flinders and George Bass, and Frenchman Nicolas Baudin, surveyed the continent's coast. Largely as a result of their efforts, it was possible to draw an accurate outline of Australia by 1803. Flinders was also responsible for giving the land its modern name (see page 33).

found it deserted, so they went to look for food. Burke and Wills died. King was saved by Aborigines and later found.

John McDouall Stuart also attempted the south-north crossing of Australia. His first two efforts, in 1860 and 1861, failed. But his third, begun in 1861, was a success and he survived.

Edward John Eyre wrote about his 1840-1 trip in _Journals of Expeditions of Discovery into Central Australia_ (1845). Here he describes his thoughts as he neared Albany at the end of his journey.

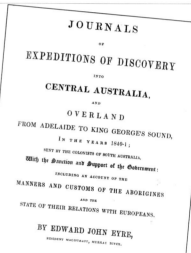

For a moment I stood gazing at the town below me – that goal I had so long looked forward to... was at last before me. A thousand confused images and reflections crowded through my mind, and the events of the past year were recalled in rapid succession. The contrast between the circumstances under which I had commenced and terminated my labours **stood in strong relief** before me. The gay and gallant **cavalcade** that accompanied me on my way at starting – the small but enterprising band that I then commanded, the goodly array of horses and **drays**... were conjured up... and I could not restrain a tear, as I called to mind the embarrassing difficulties and sad disasters that had broken up my party, and left myself and **Wylie** the two sole wanderers remaining...

Stood in strong relief means 'stood out clearly'.

Cavalcade means 'procession'.

Eyre set out with another European, John Baxter, and three Aborigines. Baxter was killed by two of the Aborigines, who then disappeared. The third, Wylie, stayed with Eyre.

Drays are carts for carrying loads.

SPREADING SETTLEMENT

New South Wales, which originally covered the entire eastern half of Australia, was the first British colony on the continent. However, from the early 19th century onwards, settlement spread. In the same period, New South Wales itself was divided into several separate colonies.

Van Diemen's Land was colonised in 1803. A year later, David Collins, the island's first Lieutenant Governor (see pages 22-3), replaced the original settlement with another nearby. It became the southern town of Hobart. Shortly afterwards, Europeans moved into the north, too. Gradually, both the free and convict populations grew and spread. The consequences for the Aborigines were appalling (see pages 28-9). Van Diemen's Land was renamed Tasmania in 1855.

A military and convict outpost was founded on the southwest coast of Australia in 1826, but it did not survive. However, a group of businessmen persuaded the British government that the mouth of the Swan River, further north, could form the centre of a successful colony. So, in 1829, Captain Charles Fremantle annexed the vast territory that became Western Australia. It was founded as a free colony but accepted convicts from 1850 to 1868, as they were needed to provide labour.

Edward Gibbon Wakefield (see page 34) had a complete theory about how Australian colonies should be run, known as systematic colonisation. The theory was put to the test when South Australia was established as a free colony in 1836. It went bankrupt and the British government had to clear its debts. However, it quickly recovered. It was the only colony to which convicts were never sent.

Victoria was originally the most southerly part of New South Wales, known as Port Phillip District (see page 35). In the early part of the 19th century, two convict settlements briefly existed there. Then, from 1834, many free settlers from Van Diemen's Land made their way to the region. Port Phillip also received some convicts. It became a separate colony in 1851 and was named after Queen Victoria.

Queensland was originally the northern part of New South Wales and known as Moreton Bay

EUROPEAN EXPANSION IN AUSTRALIA

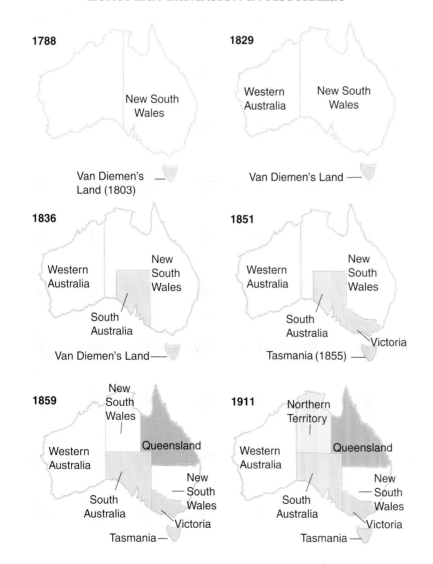

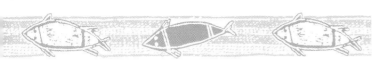

District. A harsh penal settlement was established on the coast at Moreton Bay itself in 1824 (see page 25) and free settlers were banned from the entire area. The prison was closed in 1839 and non-convicts slowly began to arrive. In 1859, the district separated from New South Wales and became Queensland.

The area that now forms the Northern Territory was annexed as part of New South Wales in 1824. In 1863, it became part of South Australia, and remained so until 1911.

The first white settlement in west Australia was founded near King George Sound, in 1826. This painting of the area dates from 1834, five years after the colony of Western Australia was established.

The unstoppable spread of European settlement had a terrible effect on the Aborigines. This extract comes from a letter that was written to *The Queenslander*, a newspaper based in Brisbane, on 1 May 1880.

This, in plain language, is how we deal with the aborigines: On occupying new territory the aboriginal inhabitants are treated exactly in the same way as the wild beasts or birds the settlers may find there. Their lives and their property, the nets, canoes, and weapons which represent as much labor to them as the stock and buildings of the white settler, are held by the Europeans as being at their absolute disposal. Their goods are taken, their children forcibly stolen, their women carried away... The least show of resistance is answered by a rifle bullet...

This extract comes from a letter that was written by James Shaw Harding to his family back in England. Harding migrated to the free colony of South Australia with his wife Eliza and two children in 1853.

Port Elliot, South Australia, April 23, 1853
My Dear & Beloved Parents and Family,
I have much pleasure in writing to you in answer to your kind and affectionate letters... My income is pretty good. We have sold a great many feet of timber to the government. They fetch it from us as fast as we can cut it... Any man that tryes for a living here is sure of it and a good one... We have sent a few parriots feathers. Willy says he wishes he could send his Aunt Sarah a Parriot. Eliza and the dear children join with me in sending their kind love to all of you.

Parriots is Harding's spelling of 'parrot's'.

A NEW SOCIETY

Early white settlers in Australia imported the traditions and beliefs of their homelands, establishing schools, churches and other institutions that were similar to their British equivalents. However, as a new, Australian-born generation grew up, new ways of life emerged.

Government schools, run by Church of England clergy, were established in Australia by the early 19th century. The first private schools, modelled on British public schools, were founded in the 1830s. Many people argued that it was wrong for the Church to run all government schools. So, in 1848, the government began to fund secular as well as church schools in the so-called dual system. However, by 1893 all government schools were secular and fully under government control. A uniquely Australian education system had started to emerge.

Anglican, Roman Catholic and Non-Conformist churches all played a part in the formation of Australia's new society. The first

Australia's first university, Sydney University, opened in 1852. In 1859, the year of this picture, its first law courses began.

Anglican church (see page 22) was soon replaced by many more permanent structures, including St Andrew's Cathedral in Sydney. In the early days of the colony, Catholics, most of them Irish, were rarely allowed to celebrate Mass. But Governor Macquarie let them build a chapel, also in Sydney, which became St Mary's Cathedral in 1836. Churches provided social life as well as religious instruction. Many people met and made friends there.

There were plenty of other ways for settlers to pass the time. A theatre opened in Sydney in 1796, where convicts and soldiers amused audiences with candlelit plays. Sports that were popular in Britain sprang up in Australia as well. They included rowing, cricket and horse-racing. The Sydney races began in 1810, while the famous race known as the Melbourne Cup was first run at that city's Flemington track in 1861. Newspapers such as the *Sydney Gazette*, founded in 1803, reported on these leisure activities as well as government business.

Wealthy families enjoyed an even greater variety of social events. They held grand dinners in their homes and on special occasions went to balls. In Sydney, for example, a dance

Crowds cheer on the horses and riders in the final stages of the 1890 Melbourne Cup race.

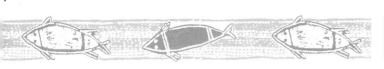

took place in Government House each year to mark the British monarch's birthday. The day (26 January) when Arthur Phillip first raised the Union Jack in Sydney (see page 22), became a public holiday in 1818. Rich and poor alike feasted and danced. The colony now had its own reasons to celebrate.

CURRENCY LADS AND LASSES

In the 19th century, Australian-born children of white settlers became known as currency lads and lasses. British-born people, by contrast, were known as sterling. The names came from two types of money available in the colony – 'currency notes' that were issued and only valid there, and British sterling. Sterling was more valuable than currency and sterling people thought themselves better than currency people.

The New South Wales legislative council asked three teachers to investigate the colony's dual education system. The teachers were appalled by the divisions that it had caused and by the poor standard of the non-church schools. The following extract comes from their 1854 report.

The Colony possesses no system of education at all, in the proper sense of the word. Primary education is divided into two great sections, repugnant, if not hostile, to each other in spirit, and independent of each other in every respect... There should be but one system, especially adapted to the wants of the country, and controlled and administered by one managing body.

Annabella Innes was born in New South Wales in 1826. She kept a diary during much of the 1830s and 1840s, as a child and a young woman. She later married Patrick Charles Douglas-Boswell and moved to Scotland with him. There she cut and edited her work and published it as *Annabella Boswell's Journal*. Here she describes the 1841 Sydney races.

The Parramatta races took place a few days after our arrival, and caused us much excitement, as we had never seen anything of the kind and were very fond of horses. We had an uninterrupted view of the racecourse, as there was only a piece of rough unenclosed ground between it and my uncle's house, and with the aid of a good telescope... we could quite well distinguish the different horses, and even some of the riders. Race cards had been given to us, and the horse we chose as our favourite was called Giggler, a very pretty creature. It did very well at first, but disappointed us greatly by bolting off the course, and so losing the race.

Race cards give the times of the races and the names of the participating horses.

ABOLITION

The movement to end convict transportation began in earnest in the 1830s. Abolition, when it finally came, was a great landmark in Australia's evolution, allowing further development of a free and distinctive society in the colony.

In 1833, the British government abolished African slavery. Many anti-transportation campaigners claimed that the convict system was simply another form of slavery, and that it should also be brought to an end. Although this was not strictly true – convicts had many more rights than black slaves in the Americas – the argument helped their cause. Further outcry against transportation was provoked by reports of its brutality. In particular, news about the horrors of secondary punishment (see page 25) turned the government and the public against the system.

There were many other anti-transportation arguments. Campaigners claimed that transportation was no longer an effective deterrent because convicts knew that they could build good lives in Australia. Abolitionists also pointed out the problems of the assignment system. While some convicts were forced to work hard, others lived comfortably. Free settlers in Australia also objected to the transportation system because cheap convict labour kept their wages low.

Many British politicians hoped for the end of transportation. Lord John Russell, Home Secretary from 1835 to 1839, believed that the convict system was outdated, expensive and ineffective. He wanted to put British criminals in British jails, which were about to be reformed following the Prison Act of 1835. He was also convinced by Edward Gibbon Wakefield's theory (see page 42) and thought that ending the convict system would make Australia more attractive to free settlers.

This 19th-century picture shows the punishment of convicts in Van Diemen's Land. Each man had to walk 50km carrying a 25kg weight. Overseers with whips forced the convicts onwards. Evidence of such brutality fuelled distaste for the transportation system.

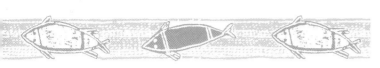

The British government set up a committee to consider the transportation question. It became known as the Molesworth Committee because it was headed by Sir William Molesworth. Twenty-three witnesses gave evidence to its hearings, which began in 1837. The committee's report, published in 1838, was highly critical of the convict system and its findings led to gradual abolition. Transportation ended in New South Wales (then including Queensland and Victoria) in 1840, in Van Diemen's Land in 1853 and in Western Australia in 1868.

Sir William Molesworth chaired the committee that investigated transportation.

ALEXANDER MACONOCHIE

Alexander Maconochie was a Scottish naval officer who went to Van Diemen's Land in 1837. He served as secretary to the island's Lieutenant-Governor, Sir John Franklin. Maconochie compiled a detailed and damning report on the treatment of the local convicts. It reached Lord John Russell in 1838 while the Molesworth Committee was still in session. The report was published and its contents helped to turn the tide of public feeling against transportation.

Caroline Chisholm (see page 35) was a passionate supporter of emigration to Australia, but a passionate opponent of transportation. Here, in another extract from *Emigration and Transportation Relatively Considered*, she explains one of the reasons why.

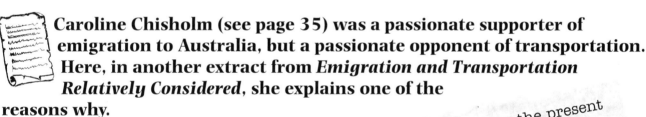

woe-worn body and oppressed mind in the Benevolent Asylum. It is true there are many bright exceptions, and I could name them ;—masters who have done justice to their assigned servants, got them their liberty, and helped them on ; but, alas ! the preponderance is too great on the other side. Mercenary pursuit is the prevailing passion of man ; what will he not do to gain this object, and what chance has the poor assigned prisoner with this bar in his way ? His case becomes the more hopeless when he finds himself in the vast wilds of the interior, shut out from the observing eye and the strong sympathy of the public.

Transportation, as it is conducted in the present day, cannot be viewed as a punishment ; for, to give a man disposed to work (supposing he is a common labourer) a free passage to any of the Australian Colonies, is equal to placing the interest of £1150 at his disposal ! A highly respectable gentleman at Port Phillip, and who is an advocate for the renewal of transportation, in speaking of that splendid Colony, calls it "the Rogues' Paradise." Intimately acquainted as I am with the feelings of the emancipists and "ticket-of-leave men," I am compelled, in common justice to a British public, to state, that the general feeling amongst them is one of deep gratitude for having been sent to a Colony wherein they can procure abundance of food and every reasonable comfort. Often, my Lord, have I heard the emancipist, at family prayer, return thanks to Almighty God that his children were not in a country where they might be tempted by hunger to perpetrate crime. Any attempt, therefore, to deter men from the commission of the horrors of transportation under the present "exile" system, is like frightening

Transportation, as it is conducted in the present day, cannot be viewed as a punishment... Intimately acquainted as I am with the feelings of the emancipists and 'ticket-of-leave' men, I am compelled... to state, that the general feeling amongst them is one of deep gratitude for having been sent to a Colony wherein they can procure abundance of food and every reasonable comfort. Often... have I heard the emancipist, at family prayer, return thanks to Almighty God that his children were not in a country where they might be tempted by hunger to **perpetrate** crime. Any attempt, therefore, to deter men from the commission of crime by speaking of the horrors of transportation... is like frightening little babies to sleep by telling them 'the boo-man will take them away.'

Perpetrate means 'carry out'.

A NEW ERA
GOLD!

The California gold rush in 1849 attracted many Australians to the USA, including Edward Hammond Hargraves. When Hargraves returned home, he noticed that the rocks in New South Wales were similar to those in California. He decided to look for gold and, in 1851, Hargraves and three other men discovered the metal in Bathurst, west of Sydney.

News of the discovery quickly spread and thousands of prospectors flocked to the Bathurst site. At the same time, other fortune-hunters began to search for gold in the nearby colony of Victoria. By the year's end, they had found vast deposits in

'The Last of England' by Ford Madox Brown. This painting was completed in 1855, when many English people were heading for the Australian goldfields. The artist depicts a couple anxious about abandoning their homeland for an uncertain future.

Men searching for gold at the diggings

the areas of Castlemaine, Bendigo and Ballarat, not far from Melbourne. From the 1860s, major finds of gold were made in Queensland, and from the 1880s, in Western Australia.

The impact of the discoveries was tremendous. Cities such as Melbourne emptied as people left their jobs, homes and families in the frantic scramble for gold. Schools and stores had to close because there were no teachers or shopkeepers left to staff them. By December 1851, half the adult male population of Victoria was digging for gold.

The prospectors, popularly known as diggers, did not come only from Australia. Between 1852 and 1861, half a million people left the United Kingdom for the Australian goldfields. Thousands more set out from the USA, China (see pages 50-1) and elsewhere.

On the goldfields, miners usually set up their tents by a stream. Next they began to dig up earth, which was then mixed with stream water in a dish or a large, rocking box called a cradle. This process

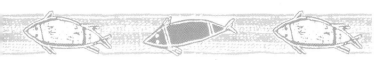

caused gold particles to separate from the mud. Many miners did find gold – the largest nugget to be discovered, 'Welcome Stranger', weighed 78kg – and many made their fortunes. However, people who set up in business nearby, for example as carpenters, or suppliers of food or sly grog (illegal alcohol), also earned a good, and much more reliable, income.

Raffaello Carboni was an Italian soldier who went to Melbourne in search of gold in 1852. His book, *The Eureka Stockade* (1855), contains the best contemporary account of that rebellion. This extract describes the troops' final attack on the stockade.

The Southern Cross is a constellation of stars that is clearly visible in the Australian night sky. It was depicted on the rebels' flag.

Englishwoman Ellen Clacy went to the goldfields of Victoria in 1852. When she arrived home, she wrote *A Lady's Visit to the Gold Diggings of Australia* (1853). This is an extract from it.

THE EUREKA STOCKADE

Gold-diggers had to buy a licence from the local colonial government. In Victoria, the cost was 30 shillings per month – too much for many miners. The miners' anger grew in 1854 when a digger was murdered at the Eureka Hotel, and his killer was cleared. Protest meetings and licence-burnings followed. When the government sent in troops, the miners built a stockade. On 3 December, the stockade was stormed and about 30 diggers died. About 100 more were taken prisoner. None of the 13 miners charged with treason was punished, and the licence fee was abolished.

Soldiers storm the Eureka Stockade, in Ballarat, Victoria.

The old command, 'Charge!' was distinctly heard, and the red-coats rushed with fixed bayonets to storm the stockade. A few cuts, kicks and pulling down, and the job was done... A wild 'hurrah!' burst out and 'the Southern Cross' was torn down... Of the armed diggers, some made off the best way they could, others surrendered themselves prisoners, and were collected in groups and marched down the gully.

[The digger] must endure almost incredible hardships. In the rainy season, he must not murmur if compelled to work up to his knees in water, and sleep on the wet ground, without a fire, in the pouring rain, and perhaps no shelter above him more waterproof than a blanket or a gum tree; and this not for once only, but day after day, night after night. In the summer, he must work hard under a burning sun, tortured by the mosquito and the little stinging March flies, or feel his eyes smart and his throat grow dry and parched, as the hot winds, laden with dust, pass over him.

CHINESE IMMIGRATION

Transportation came to an end in New South Wales in 1840. In the following decade, landowners began to import Chinese labourers to do some of the work once carried out by convicts. At this stage, the Chinese population of the colony was small – about 3000 by 1854. However, when the gold rushes began, there was a sudden large influx of Chinese men. The result was an ugly outpouring of anti-Chinese racism and violence.

Most Chinese immigrants were poor farmers who hoped to earn money to send back to their families. Their numbers rose steadily. By 1855, there were about 18,000 Chinese people in Victoria alone. Their looks, clothes and language attracted hostility from the start. White miners also resented the Chinese habit of keeping to themselves. In 1855, the government of Victoria began to tax Chinese newcomers in an effort to restrict their numbers. However, they simply disembarked in South Australia or New South Wales instead, then walked to Victoria.

The white miners grew increasingly aggressive. They drove the Chinese from their camps, burned down their tents and took their gold. The Chinese also came into conflict with the government of Victoria, which demanded that they pay a yearly licence fee for the privilege of living there. Many refused and were fined or imprisoned as a result. Many others decided to go to New South Wales in the vain hope of better treatment.

They did not receive it. On the contrary, some of the worst ever anti-Chinese violence took place at Lambing Flat goldfield, southwest of Sydney. It began in 1860, as Europeans and Chinese competed for claims on the site. Then, on 30 June 1861, white miners invaded the Chinese camps. Trouble flared again on 14 July when three white men who had taken part in the June attacks were arrested. This time there was a full-scale riot. Thirteen whites were arrested, but only two convicted.

Later in 1861, the New South Wales government passed the Chinese Immigration Restriction and Regulation Act, and thousands of Chinese people left the colony. The act was repealed six years later. Many of the Chinese who stayed became successful market gardeners.

Many Melanesians were also brought to Australia once convict labour became unavailable. They came from Pacific islands such as the New Hebrides from the 1860s onwards, and went to work on the sugar plantations of Queensland. The conditions were appalling and many died.

Chinese miners often worked for mining companies in return for a fixed wage, something most white diggers refused to do. Working in teams, the Chinese also found gold in areas that white diggers had abandoned. This was another cause of resentment.

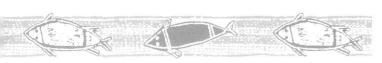

GREEKS AND GERMANS

Until well into the 20th century, over 95 per cent of white settlers in Australia were British or Irish. However, many Greeks went to New South Wales in the early 19th century, and many Germans made their homes in South Australia after its foundation in 1836. Members of both nationalities contributed to the growth of the Australian wine industry.

A vineyard in South Australia

This vivid description of an episode during the Lambing Flat riot comes from *Banking under Difficulties, or Life on the Goldfields of Victoria* (1888). It was written by a bank official called G.O. Preshaw.

A group of Chinese miners defend their camp from attack by a group of angry white men. The painting is called 'Might versus Right'.

On marched the mob, and as they neared the encampment made a run for it, and, with yells and hoots, hunted and whipped the Chinamen off, knocked them down with the butt end of their whips, galloping after them, and using the most cruel torture upon the poor defenceless creatures; in many cases pulling their pig-tails out by the roots... Not satisfied with this, their next stop was to rifle the tents of all the gold, and then deliberately fire every tent in the encampment. In less than two hours, all that remained of the camp – the homes of some 300 Chinese – was a heap of smouldering ruins.

At this time in history, Chinese men wore long plaits.

BUSHRANGERS

From the earliest days of Australian settlement, convicts ran away from their captors. As these 'bolters' lived wild, criminal lives out in the bush they became known as bushrangers.

Many of the first bushrangers roamed Van Diemen's Land. In the early years of that colony there were serious food shortages. Both free and convict men ventured out into the bush to shoot kangaroos to eat. Many convicts stayed there, stealing sheep and cattle. The two most famous Van Diemen's Land bushrangers were Michael Howe and Matthew Brady. They also looted houses and towns.

Bushrangers first became a problem in New South Wales after 1814, when convicts began to escape from the road-building gangs. They could usually depend on assigned convicts to provide them with food and shelter, so it was difficult to catch them. Jack Donahoe was a notorious New South Wales bushranger. He was captured and sentenced to death in 1827, but escaped. In 1830, he was shot dead by a policeman.

New South Wales governors made great efforts to combat bushranging. In 1825, Sir Thomas Brisbane set up a special mounted police force. In 1830, Ralph Darling passed the Bushranging Act. This allowed the arrest, without a warrant, of anyone suspected of being a bushranger. There were many cases of wrongful arrest, especially of Australian-born men who had no official documents, such as tickets-of-leave, that could prove their innocence.

Despite these measures, crime reached new heights in the gold rush era, as bushrangers held up the escorts who carried gold from the diggings to cities. In 1862, Frank Gardiner, John Gilbert and Ben Hall stole gold and notes worth £14,000 in one robbery. Hall went on to lead several bushranging gangs. The Felons' Apprehension Act was passed in 1865, in an effort to end Hall's exploits. It introduced harsh punishments for people who helped bushrangers, and made it legal to shoot armed criminals without warning. Later that year, Hall was finally killed by the police.

The most renowned of all the Australian bushrangers was Ned Kelly, who was born in Victoria in 1854. In 1877, when he was already in trouble with the police, Ned formed the Kelly Gang with his brother Dan and friends Joe Byrne and Steve Hart. In 1878, at Stringybark Creek, he shot dead three policemen who were on his trail. The whole gang then went on the rampage, holding up banks and taking over a police station. They were finally surrounded at a hotel in Glenrowan, Victoria. Ned Kelly was captured, and hanged on 11 November 1880.

After holding up a coach (top right), armed bushrangers steal the belongings of the passengers. The painting dates from 1894.

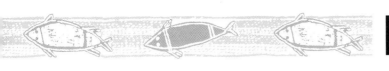
Sir George Arthur was Governor of Van Diemen's Land from 1824 to 1836. He had posters put up all over the colony asking people to help the authorities catch Matthew Brady. Brady turned the tables on him by attaching the following message to an inn door.

Mountain Home, April 20th, 1825
It has caused Matthew Brady much concern that such a person known as Sir George Arthur is at large. Twenty gallons of rum will be given to any person that will deliver his person unto me.

The police surround Ned Kelly, who is wearing his distinctive metal armour.

Cain is a character from the Bible. After he killed his brother Abel, God put a mark (brand) on him.

Ned Kelly wore a strange, home-made suit of metal armour. In this extract from *Recollections of a Victorian Police Officer*, John Sadleir describes what he looked like as he came out of the Glenrowan hotel.

Ben Hall gained a romantic reputation as a bushranger who robbed the rich while protecting the poor. The following verses come from 'The Ballad of Ben Hall', which was written after his death.

Come all Australia's sons to me,
A hero has been slain,
Butchered by cowards in his sleep
Upon the Lachlan plain.
Ah, do not stay your seemly grief
But let the tear-drops fall,
Australian hearts will always mourn
The fate of Old Ben Hall.

He never robbed a needy man,
The records sure will show
How staunch and loyal to his mates,
How manly to his foe.
No brand of **Cain** e'er stamped his brow,
No widow's curse can fall:
Only the robber rich men feared
The coming of Ben Hall.

The dawn was breaking, when there appeared outside the cordon of police a strange-looking figure, a man dressed in a poncho-shaped cloak which covered his body almost to the ground. His headgear was like a nail can resting on his shoulders. Men's nerves were excited... and when the police saw this mysterious object coming towards them out of the forest in the imperfect light with slow measured gait, striking his breast with his pistol, the blows bringing out strange metallic sounds, it is no wonder that those nearest to him were startled. Some regarded him as a lunatic intruding on the scene, some as a devil.

TRANSPORT AND COMMUNICATIONS

Road-building in Australia began in earnest during the Macquarie era (see pages 32-3). In heavily settled areas, it was soon possible to get around by road – on foot, on horseback, or in horse-drawn carriages – with reasonable speed. However, from the mid-19th century, new transport and communications networks were established that made it easier for scattered settlers to keep in touch. There were also major improvements in links with faraway continents such as Europe.

Australia's first public railway line opened in South Australia in 1853. It was just over 11km long and its vehicles were drawn by horses. The first steam railway, from Melbourne to Hobson's Bay in Victoria, was completed in 1854. A second, from Sydney to Granville, New South Wales, came into operation a year later. Soon afterwards, rail transport was introduced in all Australia's other colonies, reaching the Northern Territory last, in 1889. By 1890, the country had over 16,000km of track. The network was useful not only for passenger transport but also for taking farm produce, gold and other metals to ports and inland cities.

Women convicts travelled by barge along the Parramatta River to the Female Factory from the early 1800s. However, river transport did not become really important until mid-century, when farms and towns began to grow up near the Darling and Murray rivers. Barges and steamers regularly carried people and their belongings down these great waterways. The first steamships to link the main sea ports of Australia and Van Diemen's Land – Sydney, Melbourne, Adelaide, Hobart and Launceston – came into service in 1839.

The *Chusan*, a mail ship, became the first steam vessel to complete the journey between England and Australia when it arrived in Port Phillip Bay, Victoria, in July 1852. It then

The *Lady Daly* steamer chugs along an Australian river in 1863.

continued along the coast to Sydney, where there were great celebrations. The journey took about ten weeks. By 1858, mail steamers, which also carried a few wealthy passengers, arrived from England every month. In 1869, when the Suez Canal opened, the journey time was cut to just six weeks.

The electric telegraph, which sent Morse Code messages along wires, transformed communications within Australia and with other parts of the world. The system was first used in Sydney in 1854, and four years later a telegraph link joined the city with Melbourne and Adelaide. The 2900-kilometre Overland Telegraph Line from Port Augusta on the coast of South Australia to Port Darwin on the coast of the Northern Territory was built between 1870 and 1872. It made telegraph communication possible between Australia and other countries.

A station on the route of the Overland Telegraph Line. When a telegraph message was received at one station, it was transmitted to the next station using Morse Code.

A steam train thunders its way across the Hawkesbury River in New South Wales.

This is how the Melbourne newspaper *Argus* described the opening of the Hobson's Bay Railway on 12 September 1854.

Iron horse means 'railway' or 'railway train'.

Annals means 'historical records'.

At length the iron horse starts fairly on its mission in Australia. The inauguration of the Hobson's Bay Railway will be a memorable event in the annals of the antipodes, and the twelfth of September will henceforth be appropriately signalised in the calendar of Victoria... the shrill tones of the steam whistle will indicate to-day as significantly as if the cannon were booming in celebration of our independence, that a new era has dawned upon us.

Antipodes means 'Australia and New Zealand'.

A NEW NATION

By 1860, Australia's colonies were proudly independent of one another. They were all ruled by Great Britain, but each one had its own colonial government. By 1900, every one of these governments was democratically elected by all adult males – 18 years before this was the case in the United Kingdom. By this time, the movement to join the colonies together in a federation had grown strong.

The federation movement had begun to gather pace in the 1880s. Its supporters, such as Sir Henry Parkes, 'the Father of Federation', argued that the colonies would be stronger if they acted together on certain issues. In particular, they believed that a common defence policy would be a better protection against potential enemies, and a common immigration policy would help to keep out unwanted, non-white newcomers such as the Chinese. Finally, they claimed that federation would create a stronger economy.

Discussions continued into the 1890s. In 1891, the National Australasian Convention took place in Sydney. Its delegates discussed a draft federal constitution. Although everyone accepted its basic principles, there were some disagreements. At the Federal Convention, which met at Adelaide and Sydney in 1897, and at Melbourne in 1898, delegates struggled to prepare a constitution for which the citizens of each colony could vote in separate referenda. They succeeded. The constitution was rejected in 1898, but accepted on a second vote in 1900.

The British parliament also had to agree to the new arrangement, which it did by

The National Australasian Convention in Sydney, 1891

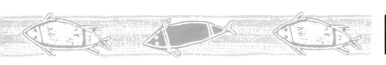

Sir Edmund Barton

passing the Commonwealth of Australia Constitution Act in 1900. Queen Victoria signed the proclamation of the new nation's birth in September that year, then sent the table on which the historic document was signed to Sydney. Amid great celebrations, the Commonwealth of Australia finally came into existence on 1 January 1901. The six colonies became states of the new Commonwealth. Each continued to have its own government, but also participated in the national government. Australia remained part of the British Empire, ruled over by the British monarch.

WHITE AUSTRALIA

Most Australians wanted to keep non-white people out of their new country. The first all-Australian government, headed by Sir Edmund Barton, supported this view and introduced what became known as the White Australia Policy. In December 1901, the Immigration Restriction Act was passed. This allowed the country to exclude anyone who could not complete a dictation test in a European language. Many white Australians believed that the country's original non-whites, the Aborigines, would soon die out – their numbers had already fallen dramatically. From the 1890s, most had been 'protected', – moved to special reserves and mission stations where it was impossible to follow their traditional ways of life. Many others lived in poverty on the edges of white settlements.

This camp in Oak Valley, South Australia, is typical of the poor conditions in which many Aborigines live.

This is how *The Age* newspaper described preparations for Sydney's celebrations on 1 January 1901.

Caitiff is an old-fashioned word meaning 'despicable person'.

...everybody has ceased to bustle and look businesslike, and is staring open-mouthed along vast avenues of life and color. The great day is here, and all that remains is to write its history and count its cost. But where is the caitiff who talks of cost? The heaviest taxpayer who looks from his seventh story window is now deliriously waving his handkerchief at the brass bands, who pass at every minute playing stirring melodies; at the walls of scarlet clad soldiers... and the torrent of all classes of soldiers, consuls, Cabinet Ministers and civic dignitaries who sweep along through the jostling, buzzing expectant throngs in wait for the starting of the procession.

CONCLUSION

The settlement of Australia began in 1788 as an experiment in the punishment of criminals. This experiment finally came to an end exactly 80 years later, when transportation was abolished in Western Australia. A total of about 162,000 convicts, male and female, were shipped across the world during those years. Their experiences in Australia differed widely – some prospered, others descended further into crime.

Free settlers soon followed in the convicts' wake. There were only 20 on the continent by 1800, but by 1850 there were about 187,000. Once the gold rushes began, their numbers soared far higher. These men and women brought their own personalities and skills to Australia and played their part in the formation of its unique character.

For the Aborigines, white settlement proved disastrous. Most European attempts at friendship turned quickly to violence as the settlers spread relentlessly across the land. The Aborigines died in their thousands from diseases imported by Europeans and, despite prolonged resistance, gradually lost their territories and ways of life.

Since federation in 1901, the descendants of Australia's white settlers have continuously reshaped their nation. The White Australia Policy was abandoned in 1973 and now half of the country's immigrants come from Asia. Governments have also introduced a range of policies that recognise and promote multicultural ideals, and have built strong links with nearby Asia-Pacific nations such as Japan.

Since the 1960s, the Aborigines have begun to assert their rights, trying in particular to reclaim much of the land that they lost. A High Court decision of 1992, in the Mabo case, finally recognised their native title. In other words, the judges decided that Australia was not *terra nullius* when white settlers arrived (see page 17), but land to which its Aboriginal inhabitants had rights. The Native Title Act of 1993 made this decision law. Now the Native Title Tribunal is considering about 700 separate claims for the return of land.

The white settlement of Australia was a daring enterprise that changed much of the continent – though not the landscape of its vast central deserts – forever. Its consequences were both good and bad and even today, over 200 years later, are still being revealed. In 1999, the country may vote to break its remaining ties with Britain to become a republic. Then a new era in its life will begin.

A Chinese market trader at work in Sydney. Chinese is now the second most widely spoken language in the city.

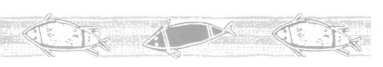

The following two documents highlight two contrasting experiences of the transportation era. In the first, Annabella Boswell (see page 45) looks back with pleasure. The second, part of a convict song, recounts the horrors of secondary punishment.

In writing of these old days, I may here add that in after years people have often asked me about our bush life, and what they were pleased to call "those terrible times", when there were only convict servants. I do not remember them as terrible times at all. We were always well and kindly served, and I can even now recall to mind the names and appearance of some of those who... were often sent out for very small offences, and found comfort and prosperity in the distant land to which they had been banished.

"For three long years I was beastly treated, heavy irons on my legs I wore,
My back from flogging it was lacerated, and often painted with crimson gore,
And many a lad from downright starvation lies mouldering humbly beneath the clay,
Where Captain Logan he had us mangled on his triangles at Moreton Bay.

Captain Patrick Logan was the brutal commandant at Moreton Bay from 1826 to 1830.

A triangle was a tripod set up as a frame on which to flog a person.

The 1992 Mabo decision was the result of a case brought to Australia's High Court by Eddie Koiki Mabo on behalf of the Meriam Aboriginal people. The following extract is taken from the judges' decision.

Aborigines demonstrate in Sydney during Australia's bicentenary celebrations in 1988. For them, white settlement was not a cause for joy but sorrow. In the background is one of the most famous symbols of modern-day Australia – the Sydney Opera House.

Indigenous inhabitants means people who were born and have always lived in a particular region.

In the result, six members of the Court... are in agreement that the common law of this country recognizes a form of native title which, in the cases where it has not been extinguished, reflects the entitlement of the indigenous inhabitants, in accordance with their laws or customs, to their traditional lands...

GLOSSARY

Aborigine A native inhabitant of a region or country. Australian Aborigines were the first settlers on the continent.

adze A type of hand tool with a stone blade at right angles to the handle.

Agricultural Revolution The major changes in farming that took place in Britain from about the mid-18th to the mid-19th century.

assignment system The Australian colonial government's system of allocating (assigning) convict labourers to non-government employers.

assisted migration A scheme introduced in 1831 to help (assist) poor, unemployed people to migrate to Australia. Money raised by selling Australian land was used to pay their fares.

beadle In Britain, an official of a small local government area known as a parish.

boomerang A wooden missile shaped like two sides of a triangle. Some boomerangs were used for hunting and fighting.

bounty system A scheme introduced in 1835 to bring skilled settlers to Australia. In theory, a payment (bounty) was to be made to employers or shipping agents for each skilled immigrant. But money was often paid out for unqualified new arrivals.

bushranger An escaped convict who lived as a criminal in the bush (the wild, unsettled areas of Australia).

chain gang A gang of convicts linked together with chains, usually around their feet. Chain gangs often carried out hard labour, such as road-building.

commission An official order that outlines a person's duties and gives him or her the authority to carry them out.

constitution The fundamental laws and principles by which a country is governed.

convict A person who has been found guilty of a crime and given a sentence.

court-martial To bring (someone) before a military court (court martial) for an offence against military law.

crop rotation A crop-growing technique introduced during the Agricultural Revolution. It involved changing (rotating) the crops grown on a piece of land year by year to improve the soil and reduce pests.

currency lads and lasses Australian-born men and women whose parents were white settlers. They were so called because money that was produced in the colony rather than in Britain was known as currency.

Dreamtime The era of the distant past during which Aborigines believe their spirit ancestors created the Earth and all its inhabitants.

Dutch East India Company A trading company set up by the Dutch government in 1602.

Emancipist In Australia, the term originally used to describe a convict who was granted a pardon before his or her sentence expired. The word later came to mean any ex-convict, including expirees.

Exclusive Any of the group of free settlers in Australia, many of them wealthy farmers, who believed that convicts should never enjoy the same rights as others, even after their sentences had expired.

expiree In Australia, a convict who became free after the expiry (completion) of his or her sentence.

federation A nation made up of several states in which power is shared between national and state governments.

hardtack Tough crackers made from wheat flour and water.

Ice Age Any of several periods of Earth's history when much of the planet was covered with ice. The last Ice Age began about 1.6 million years ago and ended about 10,000 years ago.

immigrant A person who moves to and settles in a country where he or she was not born.

Industrial Revolution The changeover from a largely agricultural economy, based on crop-growing and animal-rearing, to a largely industrial economy, based on the production of goods in factories. In Britain, this took place from about the mid-18th to the mid-19th century.

marsupial A type of mammal whose young are born in an undeveloped state and continue to grow in a pouch (marsupium) outside their mother's body. Kangaroos, wombats and koalas are all marsupials.

merino A breed of sheep that originally came from Spain but is now widely farmed in Australia.

monopoly The sole right to trade in a particular product.

Napoleonic Wars A series of wars between France, headed by Emperor Napoleon I, and several other countries, including Britain. They lasted from 1804 to 1815 and ended in French defeat.

native police Aboriginal police forces led by white officers. They protected white settlers from Aboriginal raids and hunted bushrangers.

nomadic Moving from place to place in search of food.

Non-Conformist Of or belonging to a church other than a large, officially recognised organization, especially the Church of England.

ochre A type of iron-based mineral that Aborigines used to make red and yellow paints.

paymaster An officer responsible for paying soldiers' wages.

Penal Code A collection of laws introduced in Ireland from 1695 to 1727. They prevented Roman Catholics from voting and participating in government, and made it difficult for them to worship.

penal colony A colony set up for the punishment of criminals.

pure merino A wealthy, sheep-farming Exclusive. Pure merinos were so called because they farmed pedigree merino sheep.

scurvy A disease caused by the lack of vitamin C.

secondary punishment Punishment given to convicts who committed new crimes after arriving in Australia.

security of tenure The legal right to remain on land.

selector In Australia, a person who demanded the right to select a plot of land on which to set up a small farm.

squatter In Australia, a person

who settled on land outside the 19 counties set up by the government in 1829.

steerage The below-deck area in sailing ships where the rudder, a device used for steering, was once situated.

sterling Settlers who were born in Britain but living in Australia. They were so called after the name of the British currency.

systematic colonisation The theory of colonisation devised by Edward Gibbon Wakefield. His aim was to create a balanced society where labourers, land-owners and business people all had a part to play.

Terra Australis Latin for 'South Land'. The name was used to describe the land that people once believed covered much of the Earth's southern half.

terra nullius Unoccupied land not owned by anyone. Despite the fact that Aborigines had lived in Australia for thousands of years, the first European settlers declared that it was *terra nullius*.

ticket-of-leave A document that allowed a convict to find his or her own employment outside government service and the assignment system.

transportation The sending (transporting) of criminals overseas for punishment.

INDEX